Unleashing the Power of Deacon-Led Ministry Teams

John Temple

LifeWay Press
Nashville, Tennessee

ISBN 0-6330-9866-3

This book is the text for course LS-0529 in the Christian Growth Study Plan.

Dewey Decimal Classification: 259
Subject Headings: DEACONS \ LAY MINISTRY \ CHURCH WORK

To order additional copies of this resource: WRITE LifeWay Church Resources
Customer Service; One LifeWay Plaza, Nashville, TN 37234-0113;
FAX order to (615) 251-5933; PHONE (800) 458-2772;
E-MAIL to *customerservice@lifeway.com;* ORDER ONLINE at *www.lifeway.com;*
or VISIT the LifeWay Christian Store serving you.

Printed in the United States of America

Leadership and Adult Publishing
LifeWay Church Resources
One LifeWay Plaza
Nashville, TN 37234-0175

Contents

John Temple

Dr. John A. Temple has been in ministry for 34 years. During that time several ministry options have nurtured his experience. While in college John was an interim pastor in various churches around Mississippi State University. When attending The Southern Baptist Theological Seminary, John served as minister of education at Third Avenue Baptist Church in Louisville, Kentucky. His experience as a minister of education continued at First Baptist Church of Long Beach, Mississippi. In 1981, John began his service as a pastor at Seventh Street Baptist Church in Cullman, Alabama. Since 1993, John has served as pastor of First Baptist Church in Madison, Mississippi.

Acknowledgments

Writing this book has been a witness of God at work in the lives of godly servants. The celebration of my life is to have been in His presence through their service. Several come to mind.

Charlie Bell, my first chairman of deacons—Charlie nurtured a 19-year-old pastor and helped him avoid many mistakes of ignorance without ever showing anything but love.

Dr. William Burkett who dedicated his retirement to making Cullman, Alabama, a better place to live—His commitment to visit homebound people for five different churches made him a deacon to celebrate.

The deacons of First Baptist Church in Madison, Mississippi—Their attitude of commitment and service gave practical illustration to a style of ministry that was otherwise just a dream.

My wife, Donna, who steadfastly serves in a pastor's home, always giving, rarely asking much—Her service to our son with special needs, Shawn, seems unending, yet never resented. Her support of my efforts to present this ministry has been unlimited.

Introduction

Is a deer stand the best place for a preacher during a tornado? That must have been the question my wife asked herself when she called me on my cell phone to alert me of a terrible tornado that obliterated the homes of an entire neighborhood. From treetop level, I made one call—to a deacon.

That call to a deacon paid off, resulting in 75 volunteers from our church arriving at the disaster site within 45 minutes. Every volunteer previously had indicated an interest in ministering to others in a disaster situation. Among those who responded were merchants offering materials free of charge.

The following Sunday afternoon 250 church members prayer walked the subdivision. I stood in amazement as I watched God use these people. I thought, *This is what it means to be a part of the body of Christ.* God had worked through these volunteers' ministry to bring good from a tragedy. Several families became a part of our church family and God's family. Why? Because the immediate, loving response of the church gave them hope when everything around them seemed to be falling apart.

Our church ministry teams take action at the announcement of a need. Last year one of our senior adults needed four people to provide daily transportation to a medical treatment facility one hundred miles away; 40 people volunteered. When a single adult needed a china cabinet moved in her home, five volunteers came forward after she mentioned her need in a Wednesday night prayer service. Work crews to build mission church facilities volunteer readily. Volunteers have done everything from hanging curtain rods to completely renovating homes for senior adults and widows. All the work is done at no expense to the church.

Other volunteers follow the example of deacon-led ministry teams and create their own projects. One deacon built a conference center

The immediate, loving response of the church gave them hope when everything around them seemed to be falling apart.

for youth retreats. Another church member created an Alcoholics Anonymous program. Volunteers have created several other support groups. Others have begun a statewide billboard campaign to encourage Sunday School attendance.

Organizing to Meet Needs

As a pastor for the past 22 years, I have focused on mobilizing members for ministry. Several resources from LifeWay Christian Resources have shaped my philosophy about member involvement in church ministry. *MasterLife,* by Avery Willis, encourages every believer to follow Jesus into a ministry to serve others. In *Experiencing God,* Henry Blackaby affirms that all believers are invited to join God where they see Him at work. *Jesus on Leadership,* by Gene Wilkes, encourages believers to use spiritual gifts, personality profiles, and vocational skills to serve on ministry teams. This book is a practical application of these leadership and servanthood resources.

Deacon-led ministry teams coordinate ministry to meet specific needs in the church and community. In our church, under the deacons' leadership, any church member may identify a need and/or form or join a team to meet the needs discovered within our community and church. This structure offers a means to respond to any need we discover. That response can come from anyone who feels led to volunteer for the project. Deacons help identify needs and develop solutions. Believers no longer feel pressured into ministry opportunities that do not fit their calling or passion. Our churchwide effort has broadened the resources available and quickened the response to meet needs.

Seeking Solutions to Meet Needs

Historically and even today deacon ministry has faced dilemmas in what deacons will do and how they will do it. *Unleashing the Power of Deacon-Led Ministry Teams* addresses four dilemmas common in deacon ministry.

- The responsibilities deacons have held in some churches do not address the modern society in which we live.
- Many deacons practice rituals that never produce ministry.
- Many deacon ministry organizations ask deacons to serve in areas where God has not spiritually gifted them.
- In some churches deacons are overworked, and church members who seek ways to minister are never mobilized.

Deacon-led ministry teams coordinate ministry to meet specific needs in the church and community.

Some churches seem to look to the deacons to do all the ministry. In other churches, deacons are so busy with the business of the church that they have no time for ministry. Both of these models can frustrate both members and deacons. In both models many ministry needs go unmet. In churches where deacons attempt to do all of the ministry, it soon becomes apparent that they can't do everything and are not gifted to meet all types of ministry. In churches where deacons are primarily administrators, ministry to meet people's needs takes a backseat and suffers from a lack of coordination, leadership, and encouragement. Some solution is needed to ensure that both deacons and members are finding fulfillment in their ministry roles and that needs are being met in the church and community.

Discovering Benefits of Deacon-Led Ministry Teams

Using a deacon-led ministry teams approach offers significant benefits. What's the payoff for ministry teams in the local church? Here are a few possibilities:

Deacons and members seek God's direction in finding opportunities to serve and to meet needs. In deacon-led ministry teams, each deacon volunteers for the areas of ministry in which he feels a passion or calling to serve. Deacons exhibit more excitement when they experience freedom in identifying the ministries they choose. Their contagious enthusiasm draws similarly gifted church members to join them in ministry.

Ministry opportunities are flexible, fluid, and ever changing because they are needs based. Teams may come and go or take on a new focus as some needs are met and new needs surface. Deacon-led ministry teams develop specialized care to meet specific needs as they arise. At every deacons meeting new needs are introduced for deacons to consider for future ministries.

Your church will see more members involved in ministry. Deacon-led ministry teams encourage the congregation to join in the ministries led by the deacons. In addition to other ministry areas of the church and to other needs-based ministries, church members are now encouraged to join teams led or coordinated by deacons. With deacons and other members partnering together in needs-based team ministry, everyone can work out of giftedness, no one has to work alone, and no one has to face burnout.

Deacons will model a positive ministry-oriented lifestyle. As deacons perceive a freedom to meet needs, other people in the church will imitate their example. Deacons who minister become role models for the congregation. When deacons are servant ministers, the church will desire to be the same.

More needs will be met in the church and community when deacon-led ministry teams are introduced. The goal of deacon-led ministry teams is to see that needs are met by the whole church membership, not just the deacons. This plan ensures that more needs are met. When the pool of potential servants is broadened from deacons to the entire church family, more resources are available to meet more needs. Response time to meet needs will be quicker than ever.

Deacon-led ministry teams will make the good news compelling to those in need. When the entire congregation participates in meeting needs, the church offers practical lessons in Christianity to the community through caring projects. Service that meets needs becomes a great witness for Christ within the community. You'll see your congregation become doers of the Word and not merely listeners (see Jas. 1:22). Deacon-led ministry teams coordinate witness opportunities that impact the community.

We live in a cynical world whose perception of Christianity has been negatively impacted by TV preachers begging for money, caricatured Hollywood stereotypes, and disheartening church-related encounters and experiences. Deacon-led ministry teams reach out to the unchurched as well as to hurting people inside the church. Ministry teams in your church will have the glorious chance not only to tell the good news but also to show the good news. That's what ministry is all about.

Unleashing the Power of Deacon-Led Ministry Teams will help your church move to a more relevant, fulfilling way do doing deacon ministry. You'll learn that the plan is biblical, practical, and exciting. This plan has transformed our church; it can change yours too!

CHAPTER 1

The Secret to Spiritual Greatness

Bill Burkett's life expresses greatness. Now retired from his career as a leader in public education, he spends his time visiting the homebound for five churches in Cullman County, Alabama. You'll also find Bill at a local bakery collecting truckloads of day-old bread to give to senior adults and others in need. He'll preach and teach when asked, but you'll see his greatest message outside the walls of the church he serves as a deacon.

As God's Spirit works in us, we desire to be the best disciples we can be for Jesus. Once we understand what this life is really about, we're compelled to lavish upon the world the kind of love Jesus lavished upon us. It's our mission and our passion.

Spiritual Greatness:
A Human Question with Biblical Answers

Mother Teresa, a woman whose name has become synonymous with spiritual greatness, shared Jesus' love among the outcasts of Calcutta, India. She once said, "We can do no great things, only small things with great love."

What is the secret to greatness? We've heard the question on countless interviews, documentaries, and profiles. It's been debated in universities, pubs, sporting venues, and conventions. Familiar names rise to the surface when we ponder the word *greatness*—Jordan, Gates, Lincoln, Mozart, and Shakespeare, to name a few. But the barometer of greatness rises when we capture Christ's message.

Jesus' disciples were constantly wrestling with the issue of greatness. They knew Jesus intimately, and yet throughout Scripture we read instances when the disciples would vie for position, squabble over irrelevant issues, and defend their own motives (see Luke 22:24-30). Meanwhile, Jesus continued to minister to the needy, attend to the children, talk to the outcasts, and defend the helpless.

> **"Whoever is greatest among you must become like the youngest, and whoever leads, like the one serving."**
> **—Luke 22:26**

Finally, as Jesus approached the conclusion of His earthly ministry, He gave the disciples a final, powerful demonstration of the real meaning of the word *greatness*. Jesus personified greatness—not with lofty words or a lengthy analysis but with a basin and a towel. He washed their feet (see John 13:1-20).

By washing the disciples' feet, Jesus assumed a lowly place of service that none of them would have considered. In showing such humility, Jesus' words, previously spoken on the way to Jerusalem, now carried new meaning: "For even the Son of Man did not come to be served, but to serve, and to give His life—a ransom for many" (Mark 10:45). Because God's standard is for the Master to serve the students, the world's standard has been turned upside down. Today Jesus calls all believers—especially deacons—to adopt their concept of greatness from Him and to follow His example.

In Philippians 2:5-11, we are commanded to have the same attitude that Christ had toward greatness. Christ's model of greatness means lowering oneself into service. Through this act of lowering Himself to serve us by dying for our sin, Jesus demonstrated true spiritual greatness! In the act of lowering ourselves to serve others, we follow in His footsteps. James T. Draper, Jr., president of LifeWay Christian Resources of the Southern Baptist Convention, said, "Christianity is an inversion of the world's value system."[1] When we become Christians, we are to follow Jesus' model of greatness by serving others in Jesus' name.

In Acts 6, we see the secret of greatness illustrated in the lives of seven men called to serve the church in Jerusalem. Some people complained about the daily distribution of food among the Hellenistic Jewish widows. The question was, "Who should serve them?"

The Twelve asked the whole company of disciples to choose men who were highly respected. They were to be men who were "of good reputation, full of the Spirit and wisdom" (Acts 6:3). These seven were asked to work. They accepted the role of servant to satisfy the widows' need of food.

When the needs were met, unity was restored, and "the disciples in Jerusalem multiplied greatly" (Acts 6:7). No one in the church felt like a second-class citizen any longer. Service was the solution to fractious fellowships struggling to decide who was in charge.

> "For even the Son of Man did not come to be served, but to serve, and to give His life—a ransom for many."
> —Mark 10:45

Organized to Serve

How a church is organized communicates a lot about the church. It may indicate the age of the church, the length of time the current leaders have been in place, the age of the leaders, the age of the members, the focus of the church, the expectations of leaders and of members, or whether church leaders have been brought up in the church.

Organizational Model

The traditional church model is program driven and organized. It reflects the way church has worked for decades. A "good" church has all the programs. As it grows it adds staff and more programs. It is run by the pastor, staff, program leaders, deacons, and committees. It is a model that worked well for a long time. Many church members don't know any other way to organize a church because they have never been in any other kind of church.

This church organization was shaped over time by industrial and business models. Principles that worked well in business also seemed to work well in church organizations. After all, businesses and the church programs were often led by the same people. At one time people in the workplace took a job, starting at the bottom, stayed with the company an entire lifetime, and worked their way up through the organization, gaining experience and respect over time.

Books were written about this type church as "the church organized and functioning." Programs proclaimed that they had "a place for everyone and everyone had a place." Each program had specific tasks and did not infringe on any other program's work. For years this organization included offering envelopes and records systems with six or eight points. Good leaders were well trained and trained others to do programs the right way. A certain level of control was involved in order to keep all the programs on track and thriving.

The church growth movement that thrived in the middle part of the last century was based on this model church. And it continues to work in many areas today. It is logical and reasonable. Leaders learn the rules and methods and apply them relentlessly, and disciples and churches grow.

Several emphases are evident in this type church organization:

Emphasis on position—Typically, the roles of pastor, staff, and deacon are seen as church-elected leadership roles. When people in these

The traditional church model is program driven and organized. It reflects the way church has worked for decades.

roles speak, they speak with authority. The church has elected them and should, therefore, trust them to lead the church. The positions carry a certain amount of power, authority, and prestige; but such positions also meant hard work and responsibility.

Emphasis on spirituality—Leaders in this organizational style are not only expected to lead but to be more spiritual than the rest of the church. Those who have been selected and ordained are also viewed as the spiritual leaders of the congregation. When they speak, the congregation should trust that they speak on God's behalf. Their lifestyle should also reflect that they are set apart, different from people in the pew, and therefore expected to do the work of ministry.

Any type of human organization and any organization filled with and led by humans has limitations. This type organization has had a few. Some of these limitations have been evident and caused problems in churches for a long time. Some have become more evident in recent years in the dynamic culture in which we currently live.

Power struggles—When a few people hold the power, struggles sometimes result. Jokes about conflict between pastors and deacons have come from an organizational structure like this, where church leaders do not agree on church priorities.

Control—Similarly, when leaders are put in place to ensure that a program, committee, or another function of the church is done properly, decisions must be made about limited resources of time, money, people, and facilities. Some leaders, unfortunately, have seen their job as the controller rather than as a leader, minister, mentor, or equipper.

Bureaucratic paralysis—When structure, programs, committees, and control become more important than the message they carry, the church may be perpetuating ways of organizing that no longer work. Programs that worked in the past are continued in the same way even if they no longer meet needs or no one is attending. Lack of commitment is blamed rather than a program that isn't speaking to needs. The church that takes this approach will continue to do what it's always done, regardless of whether that program continues to be effective. If it worked in the past, it should work today.

Dynamic Model

The culture in which we live has shifted in lots of ways. Businesses that once were seen as industry models may be out of business or

> **When structure, programs, committees, and control become more important than the message they carry, the church may be perpetuating ways of organizing that no longer work.**

off the list of Fortune 500 companies or struggling to retool in order to survive.

We live in an age when many adults have multiple careers and must continually retrain and gain new skills in order to survive. Few people stay with a company for a lifetime, and if they do, they may be seen as corporate baggage with outdated ideas instead of the go-to person for knowledge about the right way to do things.

Companies hire, and companies fire. The youngest, least experienced employee may be promoted to management if he or she has the skills needed to accomplish the current goals of the corporation. Employees who do not feel fulfilled often move on. Corporations that aren't meeting their goals reorganize, moving people up and down and in and out. Companies are dynamic; they exist to meet the needs of a rapidly changing world where jobs don't last for a lifetime but may even move from continent to continent.

Employees who have waited to move up the ladder are finding that the ladder is gone. Organizations that once had multiple layers of management may now have one person supervising a hundred or more people who work in teams, where tasks depend on skills and time availability. Leadership roles change as demands change. Everyone is a part of the decision-making process and is accountable for the outcome of the product or process.

The need for dynamic companies and flexible employees has led to a culture of entrepreneurs. Whether people work for themselves, a small company, or a changing company, they want results now. Most are unwilling to pay their dues to a company and wait in line for a promotion to a position that probably won't be there when their time comes.

Companies are quickly formed to meet the needs of a changing society. Adults who want to get in on the action gravitate toward those companies. Fortunes have been made —and also lost—seemingly overnight by people in their twenties and early thirties who have worked hard on a concept they believed in. They have teamed with like-minded people to take a concept or business to the next level, responding to the needs of the marketplace.

The people in the pew are changing, and churches are responding to meet their needs. Dynamic churches are finding that slow-moving committee structures, monthly or quarterly business meetings, and a few power-broker leaders can't keep up with ministry needs. Programs with rules and leaders with immutable formulas are quickly rejected by today's church leaders.

Adults who feel a part of the action in other areas of their life are unwilling to spend time sitting in meetings in the church. They want to meet needs not control budgets. They want to see a need and meet it now rather than submit it to the proper group, get it approved, and wait for it to appear in next year's budget. If a church can't provide ministry oportunities to engage people in meeting needs and using their gifts, they are likely to move to a church that can.

Such a church prospers because of an emphasis on servanthood and sacrifice to help others in Jesus' name. In many ways today's churches are attempting to return to a New Testament model for ministry through the church. The organization is flexible with a desire to meet needs as they arise. All Christians are expected to see the needs of others and to help meet those needs. The New Testament church is to serve one another and those outside the church.

The New Testament church begins with Jesus at the top. He is the Head of the body, the church (Col. 1:15-18). The focus of the church is Jesus. He is the reason it exists. He is the one in authority. He is the one the church wants to please. In the early church, no debate was heard questioning who is leading. Jesus is the leader.

All members of the congregation are equal. Just as Paul described the body of Christ, all members have God-given gifts, all gifts are needed, and all members are important. The newest member is as significant as the one who has been around the longest. Young members are equal to older members. All have contributions to make. All engage in ministry. All should be supported by the others.

With the concept of the priesthood of believers, all Christians have direct access to God. And God has direct access to each believer. Layers of control are not needed for individuals to see needs and to want to meet them, using their own gifts, in Jesus' name.

When needs change in the church and community, God gifts believers to meet those needs, and the congregation affirms their ministry. God calls new servants from the congregation. God calls, and believers answer. The level of servants will be broadening constantly as every member discovers the secret of greatness and the personal calling from God.

> **If a church can't provide ministry opportunities to engage people in meeting needs and using their gifts, they are likely to move to a church that can.**

In this dynamic church, the following emphases are evident:

Emphasis on function—The emphasis is not on position but on ministry. The focus is not control and power but on serving God by meeting needs in His name. There may be diversity of function but no debate over authority.

Emphasis on service—Titles such as pastor, deacon, and teacher are descriptions of service offered by church members not positions to attain. The creation of these ministry roles results in God's meeting the needs of the membership through believers with gifts that match the ministry.

Emphasis on diversity of gifts—God equips the saints for the ministries He intends for them to do. Spiritual gifts, passion, or calling are indicators of the ministry the individual is called to perform in the body of Christ. The diversity of gifts, passion, and calling broaden the range of needs that will be met within the fellowship.

Emphasis on usefulness—Everyone is to be useful in the kingdom. Every believer is saved to serve. Usefulness is revealed in practical love rendered in the name of Jesus.

Emphasis on expanded ministry—Two factors determine the ministry in the church. The first factor is the needs of the believers. If a need is discovered, there should be enough compassion to help. Second, ministry is dictated by believers voluntarily responding to their passion and God's call. As new needs develop, new ministries are offered. This process continues to expand since doing ministry, serving others, and meeting needs is the focus.

Emphasis on every member becoming a minister—Believers involve themselves in serving others as they grow in Christ. Ministry is not a mystical posture but a practical care for others.

After He left the synagogue, He entered Simon's house. Simon's mother-in-law was suffering from a high fever, and they asked Him about her. So He stood over her and rebuked the fever, and it left her. She got up immediately and began to serve them.
—Luke 4:38-39

The Secret Is Servanthood

A miracle of note is the healing of Peter's mother-in-law. "After He left the synagogue, He entered Simon's house. Simon's mother-in-law was suffering from a high fever, and they asked Him about her. So He stood over her and rebuked the fever, and it left her. She got up immediately and began to serve them" (Luke 4:38-39).

When she was sick, the focus was on meeting her needs. It takes the focus of Jesus on her needs for her to be healed. But don't miss an important point. Notice how we know she has been healed. She gets up and begins to serve others. The evidence that we have been touched by the Lord and have been healed from the sickness of sin is that we begin to serve others.

The secret of greatness is not in the titles we achieve but in the service we offer. As we look further into deacon ministry, this servant attitude will be the basis. As servants, deacons will be active ministers in following Jesus.

Do you have a role model for ministry like Bill Burkett? _____

Who is he? _____

What qualities make him great? _____

At what points did you see your church in the description of the organizational church?

_____

_____

At what points is your church like the dynamic church? _____

_____

In which church do you think church members today are happiest and most fulfilled in ministry? _____

In which church do you think deacons make the greatest contribution?

_____

Which church would you choose to serve as deacon? _____

Which church would you choose for your church to model? _____

_____

What would need to change for your church to do that? _____

_____

[1]James T. Draper, Jr., *Every Christian a Minister* (Nashville: LifeWay Press, 2000), 6.

CHAPTER 2

Deacons' Relevance for Ministry

If Hollywood grabbed the plot, chances are the movie might be entitled *Wild Bill and the Deacon*. The lead character, Bill, has wild hair, wears a T-shirt with holes in it, jeans, and no shoes. This was literally his wardrobe for his entire four years of college. He is intelligent, kind of esoteric, and very bright.

Bill became a Christian while attending college. Across the street from the campus is Pristine Baptist Church—your basic conventional, conservative church—very orderly and with well-dressed families complete with 2.5 children and a two-car garage where tools neatly line the garage walls. The church dreams of developing a ministry to the students, but they aren't sure how to go about it. Enter Bill. No shoes, jeans, his T-shirt, and wild hair.

The service has already started, so Bill walks down the aisle looking for a seat. The church is completely packed, and he can't find a seat. This awkward, uncomfortable moment takes over the service, but no one says anything. Bill realizes there are no seats, so he just squats down right on the carpet. Although perfectly acceptable behavior at a college fellowship, you can only imagine what many longtime members are thinking.

The people are singing "Brethren, We Have Met to Worship," but most are thinking, *Brother, look where you are seated!* Suddenly an elderly man with silver-gray hair and wearing a three-piece suit slowly makes his way toward Bill. He's a deacon, and we all know the purpose of a deacon, don't we? Like Matt Dillon, a deacon is the no-nonsense, law-keeping, straight-shooting board member who runs the church and calls the pastor on the carpet. Right? Most eyes are focused on this deacon. What will he say to right this ship? He walks toward the young man. Most members of Pristine Baptist are thinking, *You can't blame him for what he's going to do. How can you expect a man of his age and background to understand some college kid sitting on the floor?*

The church is utterly silent, except for the clicking of the deacon's cane. All eyes are focused on him. The minister can't even preach the sermon until the deacon does what he has to do. And now they see this elderly man drop his cane on the floor. With great difficulty he lowers himself and sits down next to Bill and worships with him so he won't feel alone.

The flood of emotions and the presence of the Holy Spirit are undeniable. Finally the pastor says, "What I'm about to preach, you will never remember. What you have just seen, you will never forget."

This story paints a picture of biblical leadership. It's the kind of leadership that inspires us to fulfill the work Christ has called us to do. The church isn't short on programs and models. We've always had more than enough. Some churches and consultants question the need for committees. Others question the need for deacons. Some want to add elders. And then there's the theological debate about whether the term *elders* should even be used. Other churches wish to emphasize the pastor as leader. In some churches deacons have evolved to honorary positions with little to do. In many churches deacons wonder if they are really needed.

Amid the sound and fury of church leadership models, some even have asked the question, "Is deacon ministry irrelevant?" One pastor of a mission organized his new church without any deacons. He believed most conflicts within the church originated with deacons. He thought he could have more peace by not having deacons. His experience of deacon ministry caused him to become skeptical and leery of the word *deacon*. To this day he hasn't experienced the joy and power of a vibrant, biblical deacon body equipped to serve within the realm of the gifts and skills God has given to them.

What about it? Are deacons irrelevant? Absolutely not. Never in the history of the New Testament church has there been a greater need for healthy deacons and healthy deacon ministry. Deacons are important. If you are a deacon, let me just stop for a moment and underscore this. *You are vitally important to your church*. Don't allow anyone to discount your role as a deacon. You've been given a God-sized task, and He will empower you to do this work. In this chapter we provide four answers to the question, why are deacons relevant? Deacons with the following qualities contribute vitally to the church's ministry.

Never in the history of the New Testament church has there been a greater need for healthy deacons and healthy deacon ministry.

What would you do if an incident similar to the one at the beginning of this chapter happened in your church? _____

_____

Are deacons relevant in your church? _____
Why/Why not? _____

_____

"Select from among you seven men of good reputation, full of the Spirit and wisdom, whom we can appoint."
—Acts 6:3

Deacons Are Servants

Deacons, by their very title, are servants. The Greek word for *deacon* means "servant." The word *deacon* represents a function, not a title. Let's consider some of the uses of this word in Scripture.

In Acts 6, seven men were selected to meet the needs of the Hellenistic widows. Their responsibility describes the nature of the word *deacon*.

> In those days, as the number of the disciples was multiplying, there arose a complaint by the Hellenistic Jews against the Hebraic Jews that their widows were being overlooked in the daily distribution. Then the Twelve summoned the whole company of the disciples and said, "It would not be right for us to give up preaching about God to wait on tables. Therefore, brothers, select from among you seven men of good reputation, full of the Spirit and wisdom, whom we can appoint to this duty. But we will devote ourselves to prayer and to the preaching ministry" (Acts 6:1-4).

With the approval of "the whole company of the disciples" the Twelve delegated the function of waiting on tables (v. 5). *Diakonos*, the Greek word we translate *deacon*, can be translated as "table waiter." There was a need for men to serve because widows were hungry. Since no one was helping the widows, the church appointed seven men to serve them. They met the widows' need, and the church flourished. The seven men in this passage of Scripture are known for their service, not their title.

Did you know that the word translated *deacon* was actually used before the church was established? In the Fourth Gospel, John also used the word we translate *deacon*. In John 2:1-11, John described Jesus' first miracle, changing water into wine. In verses 5 and 9, John spoke of servants who filled the jars with water so Jesus could meet the physical needs present. The servants filling the jars were known for their service, not their title.

Jesus defined the concept of servant in response to a mother's desire for her sons to be seated with greatness. No doubt you remember Zebedee's wife asking for her two sons, James and John, to sit in positions of authority and privilege. This poorly timed and selfish request presented Jesus with a grand opportunity to teach us about the nature of servanthood and true greatness. Jesus responded by teaching that the greatest position is that of being a servant. Once again, note that the word *servant* used in Matthew 20:26 is the word we translate *deacon*. Jesus used this word to describe His purpose. Jesus taught us that in the kingdom of God followers are known for their service, not their title. A trend can be seen in the use of the Greek word we translate as *deacon*. The word was known in its day as a function, not a title. Service, not position, was the emphasis.

Several years ago I was elected to serve on the state board of missions for the Alabama Baptist Convention. One evening during my tenure on the board, I received a memorable lesson on servanthood. During the banquet an older gentleman served tea and coffee. He personified a Christlike service in a simple act of service that seemed to be a natural extension of his identity. It was something he had no hesitation doing. And then he did something you don't hear of servants doing that often. Knowing that we were all out-of-town guests, he gave each one at the table his home telephone number in case we had a medical emergency during the night. This man wasn't only a servant. He also held the title of executive secretary of the Alabama State Board of Missions. Yet this servant chose to serve the newest members of the board. Greatness is a man in authority with a pitcher of tea. "The title *diakonos* (servant) applies to every Christian, but the apostle Paul also used it in a special sense for specific church leaders (Phil. 1:1; 1 Tim. 3:8-13)."[1] Deacons best express the concept of greatness as they serve.

Are deacons in your church servants? _____

Whom do they serve? _____

> **"Whoever wants to become great among you must be your servant."**
> **—Matthew 20:26**

Whose needs do they meet? _____

Do you consider yourself a servant? _____

Whom do you serve? _____

Whose needs do you meet by your service? _____

Deacons Are Models

Following Christ's example, deacons are to model what the church is all about. Whenever issues arise, church members frequently seek advice and counsel from deacons. Also, church members sometimes imitate how deacons respond to the issue at hand. Whether it is a proposal for a new building or a new idea, church members often seek the opinion of wise deacons and occasionally change their own actions.

Church members follow deacons as models for ministry as well. When deacons model the work of ministry, other church members seem to follow their lead. No one denies that a deacon must lead by example. However, one aspect of deacons' influence often has been overlooked: serving in ministry is not a "deacon's only" proposition. In the Book of Acts, the entire church is part of the ministry given to the deacons. In Acts 2, we read of a common generosity found among *all* the believers. Notice the relationship of the church members and deacons.

> Now all the believers were together and had everything in common. So they sold their possessions and property and distributed the proceeds to all, as anyone had a need. And every day they devoted themselves to meeting together in the temple complex, and broke bread from house to house. They ate their food with gladness and simplicity of heart, praising God and having favor with all the people. And every day the Lord added to them those who were being saved. (Acts 2:44-47).

The entire church met people's needs. Generosity abounded! The church in Jerusalem added three thousand believers. This big church had big needs; this big church also had a big heart. The church met needs and in a short period of time grew to over five thousand men (see Acts 4:4). Yet the attitude of the entire fellowship of believers remained on meeting needs.

When deacons model the work of ministry, other church members seem to follow their lead.

> Now the multitude of those who believed were of one heart and soul, and no one said that any of his possessions was his own, but instead they held everything in common. And with great power the apostles were giving testimony to the resurrection of the Lord Jesus, and great grace was on all of them. For there was not a needy person among them, because all those who owned lands or houses sold them, brought the proceeds of the things that were sold, and laid them at the apostles' feet. This was then distributed to each person as anyone had a need (Acts 4:32-35).

There was not a needy person among them, because all those who owned lands or houses sold them, brought the proceeds of the things that were sold, and laid them at the apostles' feet.
—Acts 4:34-35

A larger fellowship recognized the larger needs, and all the needs were met as before. The larger fellowship grew in its supply as the needs increased. The corporate effort to help one another almost produced anonymity in the sources. Luke mentioned only Barnabas, Ananias, and Sapphira—Barnabas for his generosity (see Acts 4:36-37) and Ananias and Sapphira for their selfishness (see Acts 5:1-11).

From a logical perspective the reason that only seven men were needed in Acts 6 for such a large fellowship suggests that more than just the seven men served. To assume that the entire fellowship ceased in generosity and care because this assignment was given to the seven is illogical. Therefore, as the seven ministered to the widows, the church joined in ministry.

Christian service is more caught than taught. For too long Christians have limited ministry by meeting in the classroom without teaching in the marketplace. Church members follow the example of the deacons best when they join deacons in their service to others. Deacons are not called by God and elected by churches to influence votes; they are to model care for others in Jesus' name. This modeling becomes most effective when other believers serve with deacons, not just as believers observe deacons from a distance.

Deacons easily fit in Gene Wilkes' definition of *mentor:* "A mentor is a guide. Mentors lead others through new terrain because they have been there before and are equipped to lead. Mentors model what they want their followers to do. Their actions weigh as heavy as their words."[2] The ultimate model for every deacon is Jesus. The ultimate purpose of our lives is to model Jesus before others so that they can be saved. The ultimate response comes from others modeling the Jesus they saw in us.

If church members modeled their ministry after the deacons in your church, what would the members be doing? _____

If a new church member followed your example, what kind of ministry would the new believer do? _____

Deacons Are Leaders

The biblical model of Acts 6 reveals that deacons are both servants and administrators of ministry. Deacons are leaders who respond to needs, plan for solutions, and lead believers in ministry. The appropriate response of the entire fellowship creates an attractive reputation in the community and draws more people to a saving knowledge of Jesus.

Some churches exhaust their deacons and omit other believers from significant ministry because only deacons are appointed to perform the ministry. "The disconnect between the rise of closed-group studies, which should be equipping Christians for ministry, and the actual involvement of Christians in ministry begs for improvement in this area of church life. It underscores the need for a model of doing church that leads all Christians to the practice of doing ministry in the life of the church."[3] We need to return to the New Testament concept that all believers are to serve in ministry. Deacons can help to coordinate much of the ministry that a church does.

We need to return to the New Testament concept that all believers are to serve in ministry.

Are deacons in your church servants, administrators, or both? _____

_____

As servants, what kinds of ministry needs do deacons meet? _____

_____

Do deacons involve other believers in ministry? _____

If so, how? _____

Deacons Are Partners

Deacons and the pastor should be partners in the church as they minister to the church and the community. While both serve, their roles are different. In Ephesians, Paul defined the purpose of several servant roles, including that of pastor:

> And He personally gave some to be apostles, some prophets, some evangelists, some pastors and teachers, for the training of the saints in the work of ministry, to build up the body of Christ, until we all reach unity in the faith and in the knowledge of God's Son, growing into a mature man with a stature measured by Christ's fullness (Eph. 4:11-13).

The pastor is an equipper of believers for the work of ministry, and that equipping includes deacons. **Deacons serve as partners with the pastor in mobilizing other church members in ministry.** As Acts 6 illustrates, deacons are both servants and administrators of ministry. Much of the equipping of the saints occurs through on-the-job training provided through joint projects. The deacons' examples provide illustrations for other church members to pattern their lives as they grow in more active service for God.

This partnership of deacon and pastor should not be overlooked. Nothing takes the place of a joint effort between a pastor and the deacons. Mutual respect and support give birth to spiritual and numerical growth. This is a primary key to church health. Yet another partnership needs to be rediscovered—the partnership between the leaders God has called and the church has affirmed (pastor and deacons) and the congregation. For too long leaders have not encouraged the entire church to partner with them in the ministry of caring for others. To encourage the fellowship to partner in ministry will show them that they are needed. More believers will find the joys of service, and more needs will be met.

What are a few signs that teamwork is thriving in your corner of the kingdom? _____

_____

Are communication lines open between pastor and deacons? among various ministry areas of the church?_____

_____

Does every ministry effort have a stated purpose? _____

_____

What does a deacon do when he discovers an unmet need in the church or community? _____

_____

What does a church member do when a need for ministry is discovered?

_____

_____

All of our human efforts will fall short without an intimate relationship with God. It's the foundation of purpose, passion, integrity, and ministry.

Deacons are partners. Their partnership is with other ministers and with every other believer. Deacons are leaders who serve in ministry. They are coordinators of the solution with the need. Deacons model ministry through example. They are important and integral parts of the dynamic church serving its fellowship and community.

[1]Henry Webb, *Deacons: Servant Models in the Church* (Nashville: Broadman & Holman Publishers, 2001), 2.
[2]Gene Wilkes, *Jesus on Leadership* (Nashville: LifeWay Press, 1996), 118.
[3]Gene Mims, *Kingdom Principles for Church Growth* (Nashville: LifeWay Press, 2002), 116-17.

CHAPTER 3

From Lone Ranger to Team Ministry

Years ago a college football team proved that teamwork counts. The team had an outstanding quarterback who exhibited more talent than fans had seen in years. Every week the media wanted to interview this quarterback. In each interview, he celebrated his performance without giving credit to anyone else. One week the team decided to make a point with him. For two plays in a row, the entire offensive line fell to the ground, allowing the opposing team to sack the quarterback. After that, the young man always included praise for the team in his celebration of the game.

We live in a society that celebrates individualism. It is reflected in everything from postmodern standards of dress to the outlandish end-zone celebrations we see when a player scores a touchdown. However, Christians must also celebrate teamwork.

A teacher teaches a class. A deacon cares for families. A soloist sings in worship. A minister visits the hospital. Yes, we need to celebrate every individual effort, but God's work is designed as a team venture. Let's reflect for a moment on the value of team effort in deacon work.

Consider a rope composed of individual strands. Each strand by itself is rather weak, but individual strands bound together become stronger. King Solomon reminded us of this fact in Ecclesiastes. Eugene Peterson interprets it this way:

> It's better to have a partner than go it alone.
> Share the work, share the wealth.
> And if one falls down, the other helps,
> But if there's no one to help, tough! . . .
> By yourself you're unprotected.
> With a friend you can face the worst.
> Can you round up a third?
> A three-stranded rope isn't easily snapped (Eccles. 4:9-10,12,
>   *The Message*).

It's better to have a partner than go it alone.
—Ecclesiastes 4:9,
The Message

In sports venues we've seen teams packed with incredible all-star talent who have become cellar dwellers while no-name ensembles found overnight success because of the chemistry between team members, coaches, and the front office. Champions are made when the team is healthy and full of vitality.

What ministries in your church could be improved with a team rather than a solo approach? _____

_____

Do you have a solo ministry that would be strengthened with a team approach? _____

_____

The Flaws of Flying Solo

Vince Lombardi, the legendary football coach, reminded us, "Individual commitment to a group effort—that is what makes a team work, a company work, a society work, a civilization work."[1] This truth is even more apparent in ministry. No individual can do what an entire team can. Why?

When individual performances fall short, no backup exists. When a deacon has the sole responsibility for people and fails to perform, needs go unmet. Without team backup, the ministry is like a chain—only as strong as its weakest link. Commercial airliners have a redundancy of systems to serve as backup when failure of one system occurs. The same is true in almost any successful undertaking from education and space travel to fire fighting and military strategy. All great plans have backups and potential alternatives. Successful church ministry requires redundancy so breakdowns are covered as well. That redundancy is found in team effort.

Individual performances make mentoring and training more difficult. We waste incredible opportunities if successful ministry isn't observed and modeled. We rarely see our own blind spots; we usually need someone to help us. Individual performances perpetuate bad habits and poor functioning. Even professional athletes seek coaches to help them improve their performance and skills. Political candidates have advisors to help them improve public relations. In

> "Individual commitment to a group effort—that is what makes a team work, a company work, a society work, a civilization work."
> —Vince Lombardi

ministry we need to coach one another so we do the best possible job for the Lord.

Individual performances increase the probability of burnout. Everyone experiences periods of overload or weariness. In a doughnut shop, the employees are allowed to eat all the doughnuts they want because the owners know that after a while the last thing employees will want is another doughnut. Anything can offer diminishing returns when it is experienced without a break.

If relief is found, recuperation is more likely. How many talented and effective men have you known who lost their passion for their work because they were simply exhausted? Exhaustion can come not only from burnout but also from continually trying to do ministry that you are not called, gifted, or equipped to do. Exhaustion leads to cynicism, poor decision making, and in some cases immorality. For the deacon, excitement over ministry can soon be replaced with frustration, and some may even offer their resignations. How many resignations could have been avoided if we had offered help?

Individual performances limit the options offered to meet a need. David may be a great painter but a poor carpenter. Ben may be a great preacher but a poor soloist. God has neither gifted nor called one person to do everything (Eph. 4:11-13). On a sports team, each player is a specialist. The winning combination is the proper coordination of all specialties so the entire game is played effectively. Whether it is time, talent, or energy, no person can meet every need for all people.

> **A ministry team is a group of believers sanctioned by and accountable to a local church who are committed to involvement in a specific ministry area to which they have been called.**

Does any part of your deacon ministry exhaust you? _____

Why do you think that is true? _____

How could a team approach help? _____

The Benefits of Ministry Teams

A ministry team is a group of believers sanctioned by and accountable to a local church who are committed to involvement in a specific ministry area to which they have been called. A deacon ministry team is generally a cooperative effort to minister to a specific need in the church or community. The motivation for the team's existence is a desire to meet a need so that Jesus receives the glory. An unmet need sets a ministry into action. A house burns. A widow requires a ride to a doctor. A senior adult needs minor maintenance on his house. Discovering unmet needs precedes the discussion of the ministry and the organization of volunteers.

Teams minister effectively and dynamically because teamwork pools the diverse talents of each individual. For instance, a deacon or another church member may see a need and yet not have a clue about what needs to be done. Another person might be able to meet a need and never know that the need exists. Some believers may be willing to lead but not willing to work. Others are willing to work but not willing to lead. Team ministry empowers individual ministries. Therefore ministry teams can do far more together than any individual can do alone.

Whether it is time, talent, or energy, no person can meet every need for all people.

Many churches have adapted to the changing needs in modern ministry by creating fluid ministry teams. The need for services offered by a ministry team determines the length of its existence. For example, many needs may be met in a Saturday work project; a team is organized for that one day. In a small church prayer meeting, Sherri, a single mother, requested prayer. Her home had been robbed and vandalized the night before. Using a team approach, the deacons met, and a plan was set in motion to make home repairs and help Sherri through the legal process, with insurance claims, and with replacing needed items. The entire assistance process began with the deacons but also involved some of the women of the church and even a few students. It ended when the work was completed.

"Ministry teams represent the multiplying stage that provides members with opportunities for service and missions."[2] The doctrine of the priesthood of believer encourages all believers to answer God's call to ministry as they hear God speak directly to them. The goal of ministry teams is expansion—expansion of needs addressed, expansion of ministry opportunities, and, in a larger sense, expansion of the kingdom of God. Ministry teams bless the giver and the receiver because they both experience the good news in a practical, tangible experience.

Albert Jones had a background with Alcoholics Anonymous. He had lost his wife and three daughters because of his alcohol addiction and nearly lost his life. But a friend led Albert to Jesus and took him to an AA meeting. Albert felt a need in his community to start another AA group. Because he saw the need, felt God's urging, and used his past experiences, Albert helped his church begin the new ministry and reach those in need.

"Ministry teams should focus on both member needs and community needs to minister to the flock and be evangelistic at the same time."[3] Our greatest opportunities to evangelize occur when we are not simply sharing the gospel in words but also embodying the gospel through our lives. If we love people through sacrificial acts of ministry, they will find the message of Christ to be irresistible.

So the principles are simple:

- Every team offers a Christ-centered response to needs.
- Each individual seeks to find a place to use his or her gifts and talents.
- Every opportunity to serve becomes an act of worship.

The task for leaders is to present the need and allow God to identify the servants to meet the need.

The task for leaders is to present the need and allow God to identify the servants to meet the need.

Which area of your deacon ministry is most fulfilling, gives you the greatest sense of service? _____

Why do you think that ministry is rewarding to you? _____

_____

Is your ministry an act of worship? _____

If it is not, how could it become worship for you? _____

_____

Why Ministry Teams?

Whether a need should become a ministry is determined by whether it brings someone to a closer fellowship with Jesus Christ. Every church has a mission. All Christian churches mission begins with the Great Commission: "Go, therefore, and make disciples of all nations, baptizing them in the name of the Father and of the Son and of the Holy Spirit, teaching them to observe everything I have commanded you. And remember, I am with you always, to the end of the age" (Matt. 28:19-20).

Based on the Great Commission, every church should have a purpose statement that answers the question, why do we exist?

God works in each community of believers to reach people and meet needs in specific ways. The directions churches go to fulfill their God-given mission are led by vision. Gene Wilkes defines vision as "what the mission looks like when it is complete."[4] Ministry teams work out of the mission and vision of the church. As a ministry team, deacons play a significant role in helping a church fulfill its vision.

Write your church's purpose or mission statement here. _____

_____

_____

What is your church's God-given vision? _____

_____

_____

How does the deacon ministry team fit into your church's purpose and vision? _____

_____

How does your personal ministry as a deacon fit into your church's purpose and vision? _____

_____

How does your ministry as a deacon fit into your personal purpose and vision? _____

_____

If you are unclear about your church's purpose and mission, your deacon ministry team may want to consider a study of Mark Marshall's *Mapping Your Church Strategy* (LifeWay Press, ISBN 0-6330-9440-4). This resource is an excellent tool for helping your church and the deacon ministry team to identify and respond to needs in your church and community, to determine which needs fit best with your church's purpose and vision, and to prioritize ministry needs.

Compassion and calling motivate the ministry team to action.

How Do Ministry Teams Differ from Committees?
Churches who have operated by committees may not understand the difference between ministry teams and committees. A comparison of ministry teams and committees reveal these differences.

Ministry teams focus on needs; committees focus on control. A ministry team is created to meet an immediate need. Compassion and calling motivate the ministry team to action. Churches create committees to monitor and augment the church as an organization. Policy and procedure direct the committee to action.

Ministry teams focus on people; committees focus on institution. Ministry teams are created because someone requires help. Jan, who lives alone, is recovering from surgery. Members of a ministry team arrange for her meals to be provided until she's on her feet again. The Smith's home was a total loss in an accidental fire, resulting in a drive for clothes and furniture. Men and women working on a Habitat for Humanity house can join other volunteers in the common cause of helping someone have decent housing.

Committees work the system. Some of them exhibit great concern for precedence, procedures, and policies. Committees perpetuate their existence for the sake of the institution. Despite the good they do, often the focus is not on people but on programs.

Ministry teams invite others to help; committees have set participants. A ministry team attempts to mobilize people from the entire fellowship who will respond to a need. When unforeseen tragedy or disaster strikes a home, community, or region, the ministry team is set into action. A committee might create a policy on responding to disaster. They might appropriate money for the church to help. But rarely is a committee expected to ask anyone else to help.

Ministry teams exist as long as they are needed; committees are perpetual. A ministry team can last until the person has recovered, the house is rebuilt, or a new job is found. If there is no need, there is no ministry team. When Bobby struggled with cancer, several men mowed, trimmed, and raked his yard each week so Emily, his wife, would have one less concern. Committees tend to be "standing," ongoing, part of the institution, and sometimes have no end in sight.

Ministry teams encourage believers to use their spiritual gifts in ministry to meet peoples' needs; committees make members administrators. Committee members often feel that they are doing their job if they control the budget, follow the rules, attend meetings, and give instructions. Team members are ministers, helping the church fulfill its purpose and vision.

> **A ministry team attempts to mobilize people from the entire fellowship who will respond to a need.**

Are small groups that meet ministry needs in your church and community called committees or teams? _____

Whatever they are called, do they function more like committees or like teams? _____

Where would you rather serve, on a committee or a team? Why? _____

_____

Why Is a Team Effort an Improved Method?

Team effort models Jesus' ministry. Much of the focus of Jesus' ministry was to equip His disciples for ministry. He taught them with sermons, Scripture, and parables; and He modeled behavior He wanted them to do. They learned from what they heard and what they saw.

Jesus knew that His time on earth was limited. The future of ministry could not depend on His physical presence; His disciples must join the work. As the body of Christ, we must remember that our time is also limited. Perhaps the greatest impact we will leave when we enter eternity will be on those whom we mentor in ministry.

Another factor in this model is an invitation to join the team with Jesus. He allowed the disciples to participate with Him in ministry, not merely to observe. The classroom of learning was daily life where they gained new insight by participating in God's work.

The church should model Jesus' teaching style. His ministry is not duplicated when ministers and deacons serve without involving others in the work. As Jesus planned a ministry beyond His life, we should plan for future ministry. Jesus provided hands-on training. When teams include interested believers in meeting needs, they train and expand the workforce for the future.

Evangelism and meeting needs can never be truly taught in the classroom. We learn how to swim, ride a bike, farm, repair, and, yes, witness through doing. Many churches buy resources, hold conferences, and share tools for witnessing and never learn the joy of the Great Commission because they study but never practice what they have learned.

Team effort reflects the early church model. Acts 6 talks about one kind of team; Acts 13 talks about another team who set some members apart to be missionaries, using their gifts to fulfill the purpose of the church at Antioch.

Paul frequently wrote about the diversity of gifts and the importance of all members of the body. His ministry is proof of the way this

When teams include interested believers in meeting needs, they train and expand the workforce for the future.

worked in the early church. Acts 13 begins with Paul mentioned last on this team. By the end of the chapter, as he began to use his gifts in ministry, Paul is mentioned first.

Team ministry allows all believers to use their gifts in ministry to fulfill the work of the church. Team ministry provides a way for all members of the body to serve side-by-side. Team ministry encourages Christians to recognize gifts in one another, to provide a place of service, and to encourage one another in that ministry.

Team effort multiplies the ministry. Team efforts expand existing ministries better than individual performances. Team members involved in ministry will attract other members interested in and gifted for the same type ministry. This is a great way to expand ministries, get people involved in a vital way in the life of the church, and continue to meet needs as the church grows.

Team effort improves accountability. Human nature reveals we usually do better work when someone watches what we do. Nearly all people drive their cars more carefully and cautiously when a police car is nearby. On Tuesday nights Jimmy joins a deacon on a trip to visit a lost person. The reality that Jimmy expects his mentor to participate in visitation and the deacon expects Jimmy to accompany him increases the likelihood that both of them visit. They are accountable to each other because they are a team.

Team effort increases support and encouragement. Individual performance allows frustrations and problems to persist. A shared experience is always more gratifying than an individual experience. Imagine a golfer's excitement and yet sheer frustration when he hits a hole-in-one while golfing alone. God has bestowed a desire in each of us to share struggles, excitement, and triumphs. Team ministry does just that.

> **Team ministry allows all believers to use their gifts in ministry to fulfill the work of the church.**

Review the benefits of team ministry. Which benefits are most needed in your church? _____

_____

Which benefits could strengthen your deacon ministry team? _____

_____

Which benefit would please you most in your own ministry? _____

_____

Practical Suggestions to Increase Team Ministry

Here are some ideas to help you cultivate a team environment.

Celebrate missions accomplished. Public celebrations of ministry projects encourage other members to become involved. A ministry project performed on Saturday and celebrated on Sunday produces another project in the future. The best enlistment for a future project is a celebration of a recent success. This can be done through an affirming word during worship, a video testimony of the experience, an encouraging e-mail, or a phone call. Making this celebration a small part of your deacons meeting also increases the awareness of what ministry is really all about.

Encourage team members to enlist others. Many Christians faithfully perform their assignments without anyone joining them. A wise servant invites others to join the activity so they catch the vision and join the work. A pastor may do a great job in visiting the hospitals alone. However, a pastor can do a better job by inviting someone to join him. The same is true of deacons as they serve. Future deacons can be cultivated through partnerships in ministry.

Share the need for ministry in worship. A need mentioned in a public worship service promotes more response than a need mentioned in the privacy of a deacons meeting. Mark, a brick mason, had his equipment and his truck stolen. Without the equipment he could not continue his work and provide for his family. A prayer time during morning worship moved members to volunteer to help Mark. In two days Mark received more than enough money to cover the cost of replacing his tools. When Mark's teenage son saw the church's loving response to his dad, he accepted Christ as his Savior.

Encourage members to identify their needs. Many people with needs do not wish to trouble others. Accepting help from others can be difficult. When people in need understand how others can learn and grow as Christians and find true joy by meeting those needs, they will share more readily.

The Scotts, a senior adult couple, needed a new roof on their house. When Mr. Scott recognized that many young men would learn how to serve if they had the experience of replacing his roof, he no longer minded the project being mentioned. In the church we should celebrate the people who share their needs as performing a ministry too. They allow the community of believers to minister to them;

they in turn may then minister to others. Caring for one another builds relationships and strengthens the entire fellowship.

Emphasize on-the-job training. The best learning is a hands-on experience. Ministry effort with others reflects discipleship and mentoring. Remember, the best classroom is not at the church but in the community.

The best classroom is not at the church but in the community.

Which suggestions would help your church meet needs? _____

_____

Which suggestions would strengthen your deacon ministry team? _____

_____

Which suggestions would help you be a better deacon? _____

_____

After years of ministry, I am convinced that team ministry does more than just meet people's needs. It creates an environment of ministry that says, "None of us can do it by ourselves. We need one another, and we need Jesus." We are infinitely more effective together than we are trying to meet needs alone and in our own power.

[1]From the Internet: *http://www.vincelombardi.com/about/quotes/team.html.*
[2]Gene Mims, *Kingdom Principles for Church Growth* (Nashville: LifeWay Press, 2002), 116.
[3]Ibid., 117.
[4]Gene Wilkes, "So You Want to Transition from Committees to Teams? Here's How!" *Church Administration* (Summer 2001), 19.

CHAPTER 4

Team Solutions for Ministry Needs

On a glorious Friday night, Stu and Marsha escaped the chaos of their regular world: baby food jars of green mush, Happy Meals®, and the repetitive sound of an overly optimistic purple dinosaur. With the baby-sitter in place, they made their getaway to a local eating establishment that, by the way, didn't include chicken nuggets on the menu. Since the birth of their third child, Stu and Marsha's culinary excursions had been confined to fast-food places where the choices were one of six combos. Somewhat stunned, they studied a menu that had more than 60 options, and with each entrée were even more options—salad dressing, hush puppies, fried cheese, and side orders! They sat staring at the menu with a strange mixture of giddy delight and utter confusion.

When deacons come to the table of ministry, they may experience similar emotions. Each deacon, as a part of God's overall purpose, must find his individual purpose. Too many times as servants, we look over the menu and then leave overwhelmed by the diversity of needs. If we allow this sense of confusion, we'll miss the real blessing of calling and purpose.

In discovering God's call, consider these three words: *purpose, needs,* and *gifts*.

> "There is nothing quite as potent as a focused life, one lived on purpose."
> —Rick Warren

Identifying the Purpose

Rick Warren reminds us, "There is nothing quite as potent as a focused life, one lived on purpose."[1] Before ministry can be accomplished to God's glory (not your own), you must decide where you fit in God's plan. The entire deacon ministry team should also strive to discover their biblical task.

Remember that the purpose statement answers the question, why do we exist? Having a purpose statement is important. It helps determine what the deacon ministry team will do. For example, your purpose statement may be: To meet the needs of people in the church and community. You may have arrived at that statement because your deacon ministry team decided that such a statement fits the biblical model of ministry established in Acts 6. With such a purpose statement, deacons will be servants of the church and community, looking for and responding to needs. They will not be keepers of the bylaws, controllers of the budget, or supervisors of church personnel

What is the purpose of your deacon ministry team? If your purpose is ambiguous, achieve consensus, write it down, and then get to the work of ministry. Failure to establish purpose will only lead to miscommunication, disorganization, and unmet needs. Determining purpose is too important to be overlooked. Consider these factors as you determine the purpose of your deacon body.

Make it biblical. The model of servanthood finds its foundation in the life of Jesus and the early church. Believers should continue growing in Christlikeness when they become deacons. The early Christians loved and cared for one another in such a way that outsiders were attracted to the fellowship. In Acts 6, seven dynamic leaders were set apart to care for others.

Remember that the purpose of a New Testament church begins with the Great Commission. That is a starting point for the church and for the deacon ministry team.

Learn from others. Other deacon ministry teams have developed dynamic, effective models. Don't reinvent the wheel, but don't copy what they are doing either. If possible, ask several different churches in different states and similar contexts (such as urban or rural) to share their purpose with you. Research what others are doing, and pray about what your deacon ministry team can learn from others.

Be sensitive to the Holy Spirit and to other deacons. The dreams and aspirations of the current deacons may be the leading of the Holy Spirit. Encourage discussion. New ideas will surface, and old ideas will be confirmed. Communication leads to consensus.

Ask the congregation. Deacons are servants of Christ and His churches. The congregation will have a good perspective on what the deacon ministry team's purpose should be in your church. A church forum allows for communication between the deacons and the congregation so unity is encouraged.

Failure to establish purpose will only lead to miscommunication, disorganization, and unmet needs.

Review the church's purpose statement and vision statement. How does the purpose of the deacon ministry team help to fulfill the purpose and vision of the church?

Work with the pastor to affirm the church's current purpose statement or to write a new purpose statement. The purpose statement should be written in such a way that it includes, or allows for, all the responsibilities of the deacon ministry team. After the deacon ministry team has approved the purpose statement, communicate the purpose statement clearly and effectively to the entire congregation. Don't bury the document under the mounds of needless paperwork. Give it prominence.

When the needs of the fellowship are addressed, the institution thrives.

If your deacon ministry team already has a purpose statement, write it here. _____

_____

_____

Your deacon ministry team may have an unwritten but implied purpose statement. If so, write your interpretation of that unwritten statement here. _____

_____

Does anything need to change about your deacon ministry team's purpose statement? If so, what needs to change? _____

_____

Identifying Ministry Needs

God-led deacons meet people's needs. Some deacon ministry teams never get around to helping people because they are consumed with maintaining the institution of the church. For example, some deacons meetings are consumed with finances, personnel, and administrative reports. Some deacons think they should focus on the business of the church and let others focus on people. The focus of Jesus and the early church was people, not the institution. When the needs of the fellowship are addressed, the institution thrives.

The needs of people tend to fall into five areas of life: intellectual, emotional, physical, spiritual, and social. These five areas mirror the

Jesus' growth, "And Jesus increased in wisdom and stature, and in favor with God and with people" (Luke 2:52).

Intellectual needs might include opportunities for gifted students, English as a second language for internationals, a minstry for persons with mental handicaps, or elementary-age children who need a tutor. Emotional needs might include grief ministry, dealing with stress, parenting groups, an/or divorce recovery. Physical needs range from repairing a house to a ministry to those who are hearing impaired. Spiritual needs include prison ministry, ministry to those who are homebound, prayer groups, and Bible study groups. Social needs are met with marriage enrichment, hospitality and greeters, big brother/big sister partnerships, and/or singles retreats.

Many needs or ministries meet more than one of these five dimensions of human development. Labeling the need under one of these headings is not significant. The goal is to consider a wide range of human needs. Using these categories simply help people to think of more needs in the church and community.

All believers need to mature in the same five dimensions. A deacon ministry targeting these dimensions helps believers mature in Christ and join in the work of meeting needs. The three-step sequence below assists in developing future ministries of deacon ministry teams.

Step 1. Identify current ministries of the church. Whether your deacons are currently involved in a particular ministry or are just beginning to consider a need, a group in the church may already be meeting that need. Sunday School classes perform a lot of ministry and meet many needs of their members. Women's groups, men's groups, student groups, singles groups, and others are already meeting ministry needs. Find out what all the groups are doing so that you can affirm their ministry and not duplicate it. To organize the ministries being done in the church where I serve, we list ministries under the previously mentioned five areas of life: intellectual, emotional, physical, spiritual, and social.

Turn to the form on page 73 and begin your own list.

Step 2. Identify needs in the church and community. When deacons in our church began this process, we discovered needs perceived by the congregation. Encourage members to include needs in the

And Jesus increased in wisdom and stature, and in favor with God and with people.
—Luke 2:52

community. For example, one member may be aware of unchurched persons in the community who are hearing impaired. The presence of individuals in the community with a need may indicate an unmet need that would allow the deacons to reach new people for Christ.

Your church may also want to survey the community to discover unmet needs. You may go door to door in neighborhoods; encourage church members to talk with neighbors, friends, and business associates; talk with social agencies, physicians, schools, hospitals, and other helping institutions in the area. All of these groups will know about needs. Some needs may not be met at all in your community. Others may be partially met. Other needs may be so well met in your area that even though the need exists, your church should probably not consider a new ministry in that area because it is already being well met by other agencies.

Another way to discover needs is to conduct a church forum, an informal meeting where members suggest needed ministries. The resulting list of needs usually offers similar results to the printed survey. Sample forms to list existing ministries, to list needs in all five areas, and to list unmet needs are located in Team Tools at the back of this book. A combination of the survey and a forum can be used to gain further information. Regardless of how feedback is gained, the church membership should identify needs.

Turn to the form on pages 74-75 and begin your own list.

Step 3. Identify needs not being addressed. A comparison of the lists created in steps 1 and 2, Ministries Our Church Offers and Needs Our Church Discovered reveals needs with no current ministry solution. Create a new list, Unmet Needs Our Church Identified. Any need listed on this form is currently not being addressed by any group in the church at this time. The deacon ministry team will use this list to develop future ministries.

Turn to the forms on pages 76-77 and begin your own lists.

[1]Rick Warren, *The Purpose Driven Life* (Grand Rapids, MI: Zondervan), 33.

> **The presence of individuals in the community with a need may indicate an unmet need that would allow the deacons to reach new people for Christ.**

CHAPTER 5

Spiritual Gifts and Team Ministry

Spiritual gifts are God's touch points in our lives where His power works through our efforts.

God wants to meet people's needs. Our problem is that we try to meet needs while leaving God out of the solution. A person may mention a need in a deacons meeting, and several people eagerly volunteer to help without ever asking whether God has called them to do that particular task. Although they give their best, the question is whether they gave God's best.

The best person to do the work is the one God has equipped for that particular service. That believer works out of his or her spiritual gifts. Spiritual gifts are God's touch points in our lives where His power works through our efforts. Our responsibility is to allow God to work through us. God encourages believers to be responsible for one another: "Based on the gift they have received, everyone should use it to serve others, as good managers of the varied grace of God" (1 Pet. 4:10). Our ability to care centers on the gifts God has placed in our lives. To know how we are gifted is to know where we are called to serve.

Characteristics of Working Through Spiritual Gifts

God gives gifts to every believer (1 Cor. 12:4-7). The moment we are saved, God comes into our lives and equips us for the ministry we are to offer. When Saul of Tarsus came to Damascus blinded by the light he saw on the road, God told Ananias that Saul was to be a missionary for the Lord. Paul's calling was part of his conversion.

In verse 1 Corinthians 12:5, the word for *ministries* is the Greek word from which we derive *deacon*. This word is translated s*ervant, minister,* and *deacon* in the New Testament. God expects us to use our lives, as He has gifted us, in service to others. Service is not just for pastors, staff, and deacons; serving is the grateful response of every believer (1 Cor. 12:7).

Different activities are seen in that service. In 1 Corinthians 12:6, the Greek word for *activities* is the root for the English word *energy*. When we are serving where God wants us to be, we will feel energized and excited about our service. On the other hand, serving outside the call of God can lead to frustration and exhaustion. God also speaks of "a manifestation of the Spirit [that] is given to each person" (v. 7). When we serve in our giftedness, others see Jesus through us.

What aspects of ministry energize and excite you? _____

_____

_____

A Spiritual Gifts Survey is included at the back of this book (pp. 78-80). Before continuing with this chapter, complete the survey, score your survey, and read about your gifts in the Definitions/Explanations of Spiritual Gifts (pp. 81-85). For an even greater understanding of spiritual gifts, see David Francis, *Spiritual Gifts: A Practical Guide to How God Works Through You* (LifeWay Press, ISBN 0-6330-9936-8). The same Spiritual Gifts Survey is located at *www.lifeway.com*>downloads> Book Supplements and Resources>Spiritual Gifts Survey. You may download the survey and reproduce it for yourself or others.

To know how we are gifted is to know where we are called to serve.

Spiritual Gifts, Talents, and Skills

Some New Testament students distinguish between spiritual gifts and other qualities we have in our lives. All three qualities may be given to God in service.

A *spiritual gift* is a supernatural ability given by grace to equip and empower believers for a particular ministry. A gifted preacher delivers a sermon with such power that worshipers perceive the sermon's application in their lives. What the worshiper experiences is God at work, not just the preacher. Those who serve out of their giftedness allow God to give His best through them.

A *talent* is a natural ability given at birth that is revealed in our physical, psychological, or emotional makeup. For example, Dan has an ear for music. When Dan serves out of his musical talent, he is giving his best for God. However, people who do not know God also have talents.

A *skill* is a learned ability where specialized training or education has enhanced a person's contribution. Chris has developed skills to be a plumber; Matt has learned to repair cars; John has acquired carpentry skills. However, people who are not Christians also possess professional skills.

All three elements may be present in a believer's life and should be used for God's service. We should offer our talents and skills to God to serve others. When we know our spiritual gifts and serve others by exercising our gifts, we allow God to offer His best through us.

Why Are Gifts Given?

The New Testament presents three purposes of spiritual gifts.

To build up the church—Spiritual gifts are given to build up the body of Christ, the church. The church grows spiritually and numerically. When members use their spiritual gifts in service for God, that service will enhance the church's spiritual growth.

In Acts 6, Luke wrote that the Lord added to the church after the needs of the widows were met. In 1 Corinthians 14:5,12,26, Paul repeated the constant theme that the church is to receive edification. The role of deacons in your church is to build up the body of Christ, which will happen when they use their spiritual gifts. The goal of identifying our spiritual gifts is to discover how we build the church through our service.

To minister to one another—In 1 Peter 4:10, Peter wrote, "Based on the gift they have received, everyone should use it to serve others, as good managers of the varied grace of God." The word Peter used in this verse for *gift* is *charisma*. *Charisma* means "grace gifted." Every believer has received at least one grace gift to use to minister to others. Spiritual gifts equip believers for ministry. God knows the needs that exist. God cares about people and their needs. God plans for the needs to be met by believers who allow Him to work through them.

To glorify God—In 1 Peter 4:11, Peter provided Christ followers with some guidelines for how we are to use the gifts we have been given. "If anyone speaks, his speech should be like the oracles of God; if anyone serves, his service should be from the strength God provides, so that in everything God may be glorified through Jesus Christ." The word Peter used for *glorified* means "to make renowned, render illustrious, to cause the dignity and worth of some person or thing to become manifest and acknowledged." When Christians use their

> **Based on the gift they have received, everyone should use it to serve others, as good managers of the varied grace of God.**
> **—1 Peter 4:10**

gifts in ministry, those who are the recipients of the ministry see God's power.

Which purpose of using your spiritual gift excites you most? _____

_____

_____

Calling and Passion

All Christians, not just deacons and pastors, are saved to serve. Our ultimate goal should be to bring glory and honor to Christ. When we seek God's will for our lives, we experience a calling or passion for the work He's called us to do. The goal of all believers should be to discover the calling and passion that God has for them and to serve in that area.

In some churches deacons perform their assigned duties, sometimes serving in areas where they feel no specific call or giftedness. Sometimes everyone has to do some things they don't like to do. Salesmen usually don't like paperwork, for example, but the paperwork is essential to complete the transaction so they can be paid. The same may be true in ministry situations. A teacher may not enjoy hospital visitation, but she visits class members when they are in the hospital because she cares about them.

Most people can and will do some things they don't like as long as those things don't take most of their time or destroy the joy of the aspects of the ministry they feel called to do. Simply saying we are not gifted for a ministry should not be used as an excuse so that we never do anything we don't really enjoy doing. Trying new ministry experiences, even if they don't show up on an inventory, may be a way to discover new and rewarding areas of service.

On the other hand, always working and serving in areas where you don't feel gifted is exhausting, frustrating, defeating. Where does this road lead? If what you do as a deacon is killing your enthusiasm for service, you are doing the wrong work.

All of us have seen the person who thinks his ministry is the most important work of the church. Every time he speaks, it is about mission trips, or prospect visiting, or music, or men's ministry. He has found his ministry. Gene Wilkes, in *Jesus on Leadership,* reminds us that

If what you do as a deacon is killing your enthusiasm for service, you are doing the wrong work.

every servant has a God-given passion to serve. He uses the word *enthusiasm* as his description of passion. He points to the fact that the Greek word for *enthusiasm* means "in god."[1] Service is most productive at that point.

Passion and calling to the work should be obvious to all who witness the person at work. No one can tell someone else what God is calling him or her to do. Neither can the church identify such expectations through a discussion of job descriptions and ministry needs. The passion and calling for a ministry comes from God.

Discovering your specific ministry becomes the ultimate goal. *Ministry* refers to a service where we partner with God to meet a need that furthers His kingdom and glorifies Him.

In his book *Every Christian a Minister: Finding Joy and Fulfillment in Serving God,* James T. Draper, Jr. mentions at least three significant elements of ministry:

Ministry is a commitment to God. A commitment to ministry reflects surrender to God. We release our rights and do what God asks. Ministry is an act of submission, a step of faith.

Ministry is service to God. The good Samaritan's service did not result only by observing a need in the road but also from a healthy focus on God in his heart. We need hearts both *like* God and *for* God.

Ministry moves people toward Jesus. The goal of ministry is not for the servant to be remembered. The hope is that the people being served will improve their relationships with Jesus because they saw Jesus in the service offered through believers.

Ministry Teams

Deacons can work on teams with others who have similar gifts—both deacons and other believers who are not deacons—to meet specific ministry needs. While a team may need several people with one gift, people with other gifts may be needed too. For example, several people may be called to minister to people who are hospitalized, but none of these people may want to organize the group. Someone who also has a gift of administration can make the service of everyone on the team more satisfying. Working in team ministry with others who are called and gifted and eager to work out of their gifts in service to God has several benefits.

Ministry teams teach us to care for others. Let me give you an

> *Ministry* **refers to a service where we partner with God to meet a need that furthers His kingdom and glorifies Him.**

example of how this worked in my church. Some men heard that the home of Anne, a widow, was infested with termites. The men thought that a repair effort on the house would open the door for an opportunity to witness. These men sought help by sharing the need in church. A ministry team was formed to meet her needs. After the project, Anne made a commitment to the Lord. But other blessings were created. Several men became good friends as they worked on the project. Others learned new skills. Most continued in this type of ministry after the first project was completed. The results and ramifications of ministry teams were extraordinary.

Ministry teams help us see we are valuable in kingdom work. Christians who serve the Lord begin to grasp the concept that God can use them. Initially, there may be a degree of reluctance, but once they are on task, the reluctance is soon forgotten. Churches may have electricians, carpenters, or welders who want to serve. In ministry teams these people are useful in projects that deliver the gospel in practical ways. Ministry teams discover what the church is really all about. God can use ministry teams to destroy the negativity that arises among those believers who simply sit in the pews and do nothing with their faith.

Ministry teams allow short-term commitment. Many people do not volunteer for ministries because they feel uncomfortable making long-term commitments. Unlike committees with one- or three-year commitments, a team may be organized for a day or a week. For example, after the Ingrams' yard is raked, that team may be dissolved. Many Christians learn to deepen their commitment by trying short-term projects performed by ministry teams.

Ministry teams allow a learning sequence similar to that employed by Jesus. On one occasion Jesus sent His followers out in pairs (see Luke 10:1-16). Jesus knew that God's work must continue after He was gone. Team effort was Jesus' way of developing His disciples into the ministers God needed to continue His work.

God Helps Us Determine the Right Team

Every believer should continually search for places in the kingdom where he may be involved in ministries for Christ. The process that leads to calling and passion is a productive way to know a personal place of service. This is how we know which team to join.

Ministry teams enhance the ministry by allowing believers to support one another in the same ministry. As deacons lead the way in ministry team development, they encourage other church members to join in the effort.

[1]Gene Wilkes, *Jesus on Leadership* (Nashville: LifeWay Press, 1996), 80-85.

CHAPTER 6

A Practical Strategy for Ministry Teams

Deacon ministry in your church may have been done the same way for as long as anyone can remember. Sometimes it has worked well, and sometimes it hasn't worked at all. Sometimes the deacons may have been operating in ministry teams and practicing servant ministry and leadership without even knowing it. You may have smiled as you've read these principles, ideas, and stories because they have affirmed the direction your deacon ministry team is heading.

Let's take an intentional look at deacon ministry teams and how they've worked in my church as well as churches of all shapes and sizes.

Making the Transition

It's rare to find a deacon who isn't involved in some type of ministry. Changing approaches to deacon-led ministry teams does not require ceasing all present ministries before trying something new. The following steps assist churches in transitioning from any current deacon style to deacon-led ministry teams.

Step 1. Evaluate your current deacon ministry.

Do deacons in your church work more like a board/committee or do they focus more like a deacon ministry team, engaged in ministry instead of business and control, focused on people instead of policies and procedure? Is the rest of the church turning from being committee led to team ministry driven, or would deacons be setting the standard as they transition? The first step is to take stock and determine to transition to a team-based ministry.

Step 2. Study this book.

Each deacon will want to read and study this book. In a group study, deacons can contribute from the information they have recorded throughout this book. Discuss the differences in a committee and a team approach and the benefits of team ministry. Discuss questions, concerns, and hesitations about transitioning to team-based ministry. Resolve all the issued raised until consensus is reached. Questions deacons have will prepare the presentation to the church about the transition to becoming a deacon ministry team.

Step 3. Explain the concept of deacon-led ministry teams to the congregation.

Make an initial presentation to the church before gathering information about needs and ministries. Make sure the congregation understands that this is not an attempt to place all ministries under deacon leadership. Rather it is a way to encourage ministry being done, to inform all members of ministries offered, and to begin new ministry teams of both deacons and other members to meet needs that are currently unmet.

This may happen in several ways. A women's team may have a ministry for unwed mothers. It is working well and needs no additional team members. Great.

Sunday School classes generally do a good job of visiting members in the hospital, sending cards, praying for those who are sick. The deacons will probably also have a team that ministers to people in the hospital. Sometimes these teams may coordinate their ministries, but both teams can continue to care for people who are hospitalized.

An unmet need may be to help people move. A church in a university town, near a military base, or in a city with businesses that transfer people could offer a ministry to help people move. A deacon might decide to partner with another man in the congregation to set up this team to help whenever needed. Men and women join the team to provide transportation, pack and unpack boxes, move heavy furniture, and to prepare food for the day of the move.

The goal is to engage the congregation with the energy and enthusiasm that comes with the opportunity to serve others and meet needs. The transition to a deacon ministry team is not about control but about expanded ministry.

Step 4. Research ministries and needs.

Gather information about needs, current ministries, and unmet needs.

The transition to a deacon ministry team is not about control but about expanded ministry.

Look for a balanced approach that includes meeting emotional, physical, social, spiritual, and intellectual needs.

Step 5. Identify spiritual gifts, skills, talents.
In small groups, individually, on retreats, or in other ways, encourage all church members, including deacons, to discover their spiritual gifts. Encourage those who have previously taken a spiritual gifts inventory to do so again to see if they discover any new insight or the same gifts are recognized and affirmed. In addition to spiritual gifts, consider people's skills, talents, passion, and calling.

Step 6. Prioritize needs.
Using the church's purpose and vision statements and the deacon ministry team's purpose statement, review current ministries and perceived needs. The entire congregation will need to have input in this process. Some ministries may no longer be needed; others will continue; and others will begin. Together a church may decide that a ministry is no longer needed, no longer effective, or no longer fits the purpose and vision of the church. Together a church will decide to rechannel those resources into another ministry. Since meeting needs is the responsibility of the entire community of believers, the deacons will not want to make such decisions in isolation.

Step 7. Consider and select new ministries.
The church will likely discover a number of unmet needs and potential ministries. Before beginning a new ministry, determine whether it fits into the purpose and vision of the church and whether two or more people feel equipped and called to begin a team.

Ministry teams will come and go. Not beginning a team right now to address a specific need does not mean that such a team will not be started in the future when people are called and gifted to form a team to begin that ministry.

To insist on having deacons lead all teams is to put all deacons in leadership or administrative roles for which many do not feel called or gifted.

Step 8. Announce new ministry teams and invite members to join.
Remember that all teams will not be led by deacons. To insist on having deacons lead all teams is to put all deacons in leadership or administrative roles for which many do not feel called or gifted. In

fact, some needs may be discovered and teams formed with no deacons on the team. The deacon ministry team should encourage and support all members in finding ways to form ministry teams to meet needs in the church and community.

Step 9. Assess needs for training.

Teams may be formed to teach English as a second language, teach computer skills, repair automobiles, tutor elementary-age children, provide construction teams in other countries, or provide grief ministry. All of these teams can benefit from training. Learning and planning together can help build the team.

Step 10. Evaluate

Teams will come and go. Needs will change. People's gifts, skills, and talents will need to be redirected for ministry use. Team ministry is dynamic. Needs never cease, but they do change over time. When people are excited about participating in ministry, they will not want to be members of teams that do nothing.

From time to time a new survey may be needed to assess needs. Continue to look for opportunities to serve God and those in the church and community.

Team ministry is rewarding. The deacons on the deacon ministry team will know the joys of serving God and meeting needs. Your best days of deacon ministry are just ahead.

Developing a Ministry Teams Manual

Creating a manual with information about all ministry teams—both those led by deacons and other ministry teams—increases understanding and effectiveness for deacon-led ministry teams. This notebook should contain all the ministries the church currently has. Each ministry team should have information in the manual that include:

- A definition or explanation of the scope of that team's work
- The target group to receive the ministry
- The types of activities the teams does
- A team leader and/or contact person
- A list of people currently involved, with names, addresses, phone numbers, and e-mail addresses
- Procedures, forms, and guidelines

This manual will help deacons:
- Stay informed about all the church's ministries.
- Serve as a resource for the deacon to assist people in finding any ministry help they need.
- Refer new members, new deacons, and other church members to ministry teams where they can use their gifts.

If your church has procedures or processes for ministry teams, forms they will need, or other guidelines, current samples of all of these should be included in the manual. For example, forms may be needed to record ministry actions or to request funds.

The ministry team manual will need to be updated at least annually. As deacons rotate on and off the deacon ministry team, ministry team members change, and ministry teams come and go, the manual will be a useful resource to help your church focus on ministry.

Thinking in Different Directions

The best organizational structure for the deacon ministry team (all elected deacons) is tailored according to the team's purpose, needs of the church and community, strategies, resources available, and coaching required. For instance, the key roles of leaders in a team approach to deacon ministry are coordinating, training, equipping, and supporting. These are the roles and responsibility of a coach. Most deacons will also find themselves in the role of player/coach as they lead and participate within their God-given talents, gifts, and calling.

A multiple team structure calls for a different approach to organization. Churches with multiple ministries require greater attention to coordination and planning than churches with fewer ministries. Churches may coordinate ministries in several ways. The chairman of deacons can perform the task or a representative leadership team can be formed. As long as the church and the deacons have only a few ministry teams, the deacon chairman can probably coordinate the ministries. As ministry teams expand in number, a leadership team becomes necessary. The leader of the deacon ministry team becomes a coordinator, a player/coach, and an equipper. Here are a few things to note about this approach to deacon ministry:
- As the number of deacon-led ministry teams grows, a deacon leadership team needs to be formed in order to take care of the responsibilities of planning and coordination.

The key roles of leaders in a team approach to deacon ministry are coordinating, training, equipping, and supporting.

53

- This model suggests a degree of equality and authority among the teams.
- Teams are highly autonomous yet accountable.
- Teams are formed around the calling, ministry, and gifts of the members.
- Some teams within the church may overlap. They may even have common members. Other teams may have different roles but find themselves ministering to the same families or individuals. These teams need to share information and coordinate tasks.
- Some teams function apart from or with little relationship with other teams.
- Some teams are large and some are small.

The Deacon Ministry Leadership Team
A deacon ministry leadership team (the elected leaders—formerly officers—of the deacons) coordinates the overall deacon ministry. The purpose of this leadership team is to coordinate the ministries performed. Team leaders for those ministries serve as representatives on the leadership team.

The deacon ministry leadership team is selected by the deacons from the deacons currently. Ministry coordinators (team leaders for various deacon-led ministry teams) need spiritual gifts and interests in the ministry areas they coordinate.

Responsibilities of Deacon Leadership Team Members
The size of the deacon body, the spiritual gifts of individual deacons, and the needs of the church and community, and the number of deacon-led ministry teams determine how many leaders are needed for the overall work of the deacons in your church. You may use term "team leader" or "deacon chairman," whichever is more comfortable in your church. Add assistants as needed. The following list of responsibilities of deacon leadership positions are presented as a beginning point for developing a team ministry with the deacons. You will want to modify these to reflect more accurately your specific situation. However you define your deacon leadership positions, the concept of guiding ministry teams with diverse responsibilities is the focus.

Tasks of deacon ministry team leaders include:
- Preside over all general deacon ministry team meetings.

- Plan and lead deacon leadership team meetings.
- Guide deacons in developing or reviewing the church's deacon ministry purpose statement.
- Guide the process of identifying needs to be met.
- Guide deacon-led ministry teams to provide the ministries desired.
- Represent deacons in other ministries within the church.
- Maintain a ministry teams manual.
- Record proceedings of all deacons meetings.
- Record proceedings of deacon ministry team leadership (officers) meetings.

Ministry Team Leaders Responsibilities
- Convene deacons as a team in the minstry/need area identified.
- Present ministry opportunities and encourage deacons to volunteer for the ministry God is calling them to lead or serve.
- Communicate information, needs and ministry opportunities to team members.
- Keep records as needed.
- Provide training as needed.
- Enlist volunteers as needed.
- Coordinate ministry actions.

Selection of Team Leaders
One of the most important aspects of functioning ministry teams is to have good leaders. Each team may select its own leader. Leadership ability, experience with the specific ministry, and motivation to lead should be considered. Teams may or may not be led by deacons.

Mentoring New Deacons
Each year deacon orientation should be provided for all new deacons. At that meeting, every new deacon should learn about the various ministry teams and opportunities for service. In addition, expectations, meeting dates, introduction of leaders, and general explanation of the deacon ministry team should be offered. In our deacon orientation class, we discuss the importance of all deacons using the church's prayer room. We learn about confidentiality. New deacons need this help, but newly elected deacons who have served before also benefit

from the orientation. Because ministry teams change, all newly elected deacons benefit from an orientation.

All new (first-time) deacons benefit from having a mentor. Each new deacon can be teamed with an experienced deacon, preferably with someone who serves in the same ministry area. The experienced deacon can help the new deacon learn the ropes and avoid the traps. A comfort zone around a new deacon will help him minister more quickly. Multiple mentors are possible. A new deacon may have someone to show him how to visit hospitals and someone else to show him how to visit prospects.

Two important aspects of mentoring are encouragement and training. Never assume a new deacon knows how to do the work. A caring environment where deacons can ask for help and see positive reinforcement for effort is important. Many deacons want to do better, but they don't know how and are afraid to ask. We should anticipate their questions, endorse their efforts, and allow them to learn as they serve.

Other Deacon Responsibilities

Some of the responsibilities deacons have assumed in the past may still be assigned to the deacon ministry team—in addition to meeting ministry needs.

Lord's Supper

Deacons can continue to plan and prepare for the Lord's Supper. A special team may be formed to do this, or deacons may help on a rotating basis.

Administration

Deacons with gifts in leadership and administration are still needed on the deacon ministry team. Deacons with such gifts may lead teams and/or serve on the deacon ministry leadership team.

Deacon-led Ministry Team Meetings

As deacons turn their focus to providing ministry to meet needs, the agenda of your deacons meetings will also change. Focusing on ministry and the work of the ministry teams in regularly scheduled meetings will encourage a greater focus on needs and a lesser focus on administration. Consider the following three-part outline:

1. Discuss people first and problems later. Discussion of last month's ministry activity and the need for helping others next month is the first topic after prayer and devotion.

Remember that individual ministry teams do not need to meet every month. Ministry teams will determine their own schedules. More meetings may be needed near the first of the year when new ministries are beginning. After that the teams will only meet occasionally. Ministry teams do not need to wait for the regularly scheduled deacon ministry team meeting to meet; they can meet whenever they wish to get together. Team meetings can be as frequent and flexible as needed.

2. Introduce new ministry needs at every monthly deacons meeting. This provides the opening for new ministries to be suggested. As long as two people can be found to lead the work, the ministry may be planned. The two people do not need to be deacons. If the ministry is needed, deacons may turn to the congregation to form a team to meet the need.

3. Celebrate ministry. Ministry activity should be celebrated in the deacons meeting and in the church itself. Celebration aids visibility. People want to participate in meaningful ministry that the church celebrates. Celebrating what was done last Saturday will assure something else is done next Saturday.

If you have asked members of the congregation to volunteer, use them. After all, the ultimate goal of deacon-led ministry teams is not just to mobilize deacons. The goal is to mobilize Christ's entire church to take care of His entire church—and the whole world. May God find us doing so when He returns!

CHAPTER 7

How to Mobilize Believers for Ministry

Therefore, brothers, by the mercies of God, I urge you to present your bodies as a living sacrifice, holy and pleasing to God; this is your spiritual worship. Do not be conformed to this age, but be transformed by the renewing of your mind, so that you may discern what is the good, pleasing, and perfect will of God.
—Romans 12:1-2

Biblical believers personify ministry. They realize that church is not another calendar item permanently etched on Sundays and Wednesday nights. They are Romans 12:1-2 in the flesh, placing themselves on the altar as living sacrifices.

Join me for a quick tour of our church in progress. Step into our church library where a church library ministry team member dusts the library shelves to improve the look of the church library. Now let's travel to a small landing strip across town as a pilot, a member of our church, is preparing to make a mercy flight for someone in need of medical attention.

Now let's crisscross to the community mission where a retired couple is collecting furniture and clothing to help with needy people in the county. And then let's make a quick return to the church building where a young mother is updating the bulletin boards in the prayer room.

We aren't done yet. Let's check on a doctor here in town who is making travel arrangements for this summer's medical mission trip to Guatemala. Perhaps more "church" occurred on this Tuesday than on Sunday.

The goal of deacon-led ministry teams is to mobilize not only the deacons but the entire community of believers to do ministry. New teams formed to meet newly discovered unmet needs are under the deacon's leadership, but other interested believers are encouraged to join the team. Imagine your entire fellowship serving God by becoming ministers to one another—and to the community. How can that happen? First, we need to motivate deacons. Then we can focus on mobilizing members.

Principles for Motivating Deacons

We begin mobilizing church members by motivating deacons. When is a deacon in his element? Many church members would answer that the deacon is in his element when he's in front of the church five minutes before the Sunday School bell rings or when he is in a highly volatile meeting. In truth, a biblical deacon is in his element when he is ministering. Motivating deacons involves two principles: focusing on calling as well as passion and teaming with others.

Motivate Deacons by Focusing on Gifts, Calling, and Passion

If you want to see ministry production and high morale in your ministry efforts, begin by allowing deacons to serve in areas where they are gifted and called. To know how deacons are gifted reveals where they are called in ministry. A spiritual gifts survey will help them understand where the Holy Spirit has equipped them for ministry. Deacons may want t complete the survey every year or every time they are elected. Taking this survey more than once may verify previous results and may offer new insights. The goal of the survey is to discover the types of ministry best suited for each believer.

A Spiritual Gifts Survey is located at *www.lifeway.com*>downloads>Book Supplements and Resources>Spiritual Gifts Survey. You may download and reproduce this survey instrument.

After deacons walk through the process of discovering their gifts, calling, and passion, the church can match up the needs to team members and ministry teams. Looking at the church's needs—both past and present—is a great place to begin the process of developing a ministry team strategy. Little pressure should be applied to cover all ministries because God calls out volunteers for the ministries He wants performed. Forcing deacons to serve beyond God's calling leads to burnout and inadequate ministry.

Keep in mind that volunteering for ministry should grow out of the expression of passion or calling each deacon feels in his heart as he discusses the needs for ministry. Such a discussion allows God to call out deacons who are to lead the ministry.

Although the emphasis is on spiritual gifts, passion, and calling, remember that these attributes are more clearly verified by serving. Our best deacon candidates are men who are already involved in serving. In other words, pay more attention to a man's track record than to his aptitude. Also keep in mind that asking each deacon to lead in only one ministry often results in better training and more intense focus for that ministry.

In the church I serve, two deacons coordinate hospital ministry. Initially these two men joined me as I mentored them in hospital visitation. Before we went into a room, we talked about the condition of the person, the Scripture we would read, and the type of prayer we would offer. In a few short weeks, these two deacons became proficient in visiting hospitals and capable of training others to do the same. Because hospital visitation is their one focus, they have become experts in their ministry.

Motivate Deacons by Training Others in Ministry Efforts

One important standard for a ministry team is the requirement of at least two volunteers for any ministry area. Why? Team effort increases the awareness that someone knows the work is being done. Team effort also increases encouragement and support by making the responsibility, the frequency, and the burden less overwhelming. Team effort decreases the negative aspects of ownership and control.

Also keep in mind that the church is already doing many ministries well. Some of those ministry teams may welcome deacons to join their teams. Not every ministry team must be led by a deacon. Someone with a combination of gifts that include administration may lead a team, while a deacon may choose to be an active member of the team. To make all deacons team leaders would continue to force an administrative role on deacons that many are not gifted to do or passionate about doing.

Deacons may assist in any and all church ministries where they are needed or invited to serve. To assist means they will not be concerned with leadership, recruitment, or training, but they will help when needed with the actual work. Like other church members, deacons should be allowed to join other believers in ministry teams to meet people's needs in Christ's name.

Another important standard for ministry comes when a team first meets. Each team needs to clarify the needs the team will address and develop specific individual and team responsibilities.

Deacons need to be motivated to minister. But after we motivate deacons, we still need to mobilize other church members.

What motivates you to serve? _____

_____

How would you encourage someone else to join in ministry, based on what motivates you?_____

_____

What training would help you feel more equipped to minister?

_____

Five Steps in Mobilizing Believers

One significant goal of deacon service is to mobilize the entire fellowship in ministry to others. The biblical model of the New Testament church encourages believers to care for others (see 1 Cor. 12:4-7). The following steps enhance member involvement:

Step 1. Communicate the plan.

As a pastor, I've learned that Christians help more when they understand what is being done. Whether you're using public announcements in worship services, church newsletter articles, prayer requests, church discussions, personal invitation by deacons, pastoral affirmation of the work, or celebration of joint efforts, communicate the plan.

Step 2. Identify people's value to the work.

An effective deacon invites members to participate in serving God and meeting needs. Seize every available opportunity to encourage members to discover their spiritual gifts and to identify their passions or callings as the deacons have done. The process described in mobilizing deacons could be repeated in small groups such as Bible study classes, support groups, prayer groups, accountability groups, or any other setting where interaction is possible.

Step 3. Invite volunteers to join a ministry.

Members discover a new sense of value and worth when they join in the work. For example, a new church member may feel included if invited to help distribute bulletins on Sunday morning. Deacons leading a ministry should be enlisting others as they fellowship with them. Here are four ideas that can multiply your efforts to mobilize the members.

> Now there are different gifts, but the same Spirit. There are different ministries, but the same Lord.
> 1 Corinthians 12:4-5

- Allow members to discuss possible needs in a church forum.
- Conduct a job fair to advertise what services are available.
- Offer regular opportunities for members to be involved in short-term projects.
- Delegate responsibility to members whenever possible.

Celebrate projects as they are completed, and future projects will find greater support.

Step 4. Train and coordinate.

To include more members in the various ministries of the church, deacons must shift their focus from performing the work to coordinating the work. The first step in coordinating is training volunteers. Training helps to ensure the ministry is performed in a reliable way and to avoid the frustration of new workers who aren't comfortable with their ministry.

Training should be a requirement prior to approval as a worker. To make the training a part of the enlistment tests commitment and improves attendance. Creating a written training procedure that can be reproduced from year to year improves the process.

Good training includes apprenticeships where new workers are linked with experienced laborers who model the ministry and encourage the new volunteer. The yokefellow ministry (a common ministry for younger men or for those who don't match the biblical or church qualifications for a deacon) may be perceived as a part of this training. Having yokefellows aligned with deacons expands the workforce and provides a teaching platform for future deacons to learn the work. (For more information on yokefellows, see Henry Webb, *Deacons: Servant Models in the Church, Updated Edition,* pages 86-87, [Broadman & Holman, ISBN 0-0854-2463-6].)

Step 5. Celebrate!

Celebrate projects as they are completed, and future projects will find greater support. Celebration can include private or personal affirmation to the members who helped. Celebration could be a party at the end of a project. Even a cup of coffee before going home can be an occasion to communicate appreciation and encouragement to workers. A thank-you note after a project is finished communicates appreciation that lingers beyond the workday and shares personal feelings often not expressed in public. This celebration might also include a fellowship at the end of the year.

To keep the celebration on a spiritually mature level, focus on serving the Lord and seeking His approval, not the approval of other people. Aiming the service toward God and considering service as an offering of sacrifice for God lessens the temptation to become selfish in the celebration.

"OK, I'm convinced of the necessity of motivating deacons and mobilizing believers," you may say. "But our church has problems when we attempt to develop a ministering church. What are some keys to help my church?"

Which of these five steps does your deacon ministry team do well? _____

_____

Which areas need improvement? _____

_____

_____

_____

CHAPTER 8

Keys to Developing a Ministering Church

Once you have made the transition from a committee mind-set to a teams ministry approach, you will see a dramatic change in the energy level among those who have found their place of service and discovered the joy and fulfillment of using their gifts in ministry. Their excitement will be contagious. More people will want to find places to serve.

The pastor and deacons will play a significant role in keeping the momentum going. No ministry is immune to the threat of disconnection. So how do you keep members from slowly drifting out of ministry? Let's look at six keys to help your members discover the joy and benefits of becoming a ministering church. Each key focuses on a specific solution to handle a barrier that addresses a cause of inactivity.

Key 1. Spiritual maturity defeats worldliness.

For we are God's co-workers. You are God's field, God's building.
1 Corinthians 3:9

Worldliness is an outlook on life that bases values, morals, and priorities on the standards of the culture. Ananias and Sapphira allowed money to supercede their compassion for widows (Acts 5:1-11). In 1 Corinthians, Paul wrote about immature Christians in strife and conflict, living like unbelievers (1 Cor. 3:1-23). Transforming new believers' focus from the world's way to God's way takes time.

There are multiple symptoms of worldliness. *Materialism* is a focus on the physical rather than the spiritual side of life. *Selfishness* is a focus on "what I receive" instead of "what I give." *Rights* is a focus on freedoms over responsibility for others. *Relativism* is a value system of right and wrong based on society's standards. These are common priorities in our society. In the secular world we compare what we have with what others possess. We demand our way and clamor for favor and privilege. However, materialism, selfishness, rights, and relativism should not be common expectations in the kingdom of God. New

Christians need time for God to help them change their focus.

Worldliness expresses itself in several spiritual consequences. A lack of conviction is evident when Christians are unsettled on absolutes. When Christians are not well rooted in Scripture, jealousy, unbelief, and quarreling may be the fruit of their labor. A lack of commitment results from allegiance to former lifestyles. A commitment to Bible study and worship exceeds what many believers offer to the Lord. A lack of unity stems from selfishness, and a claim of "rights" causes competition.

Spiritual maturity overcomes worldliness. Spiritual maturity is a level of walking with God where God is the only source of values, morals, and priorities in life. Paul described spiritual maturity this way:

> Pay careful attention, then, to how you walk—not as unwise people but as wise—making the most of the time, because the days are evil. So don't be foolish, but understand what the Lord's will is. And don't get drunk with wine, which leads to reckless actions, but be filled with the Spirit: speaking to one another in psalms, hymns, and spiritual songs, singing and making music to the Lord in your heart, giving thanks always for everything to God the Father in the name of our Lord Jesus Christ, submitting to one another in the fear of Christ (Eph. 5:15-21).

**Don't be foolish, but understand what the Lord's will is.
—Ephesians 5:17**

Paul was challenging the church to grow up! Worship and experiencing God every day of our lives will escort us into a new level of spiritual maturity. Spiritual maturity changes our focus. We take on the mind of Christ. Although difficult to quantify, spiritual maturity includes four factors: fruit of the Spirit, spiritual wisdom, tested faith, and consistent lifestyle.

The fruit of the Spirit is love, joy, peace, patience, kindness, goodness, faith, gentleness, and self-control (Gal. 5:22-23). Each of these attributes reflects in a life focused on God. As God's Spirit controls our lives, we experience less of the world's influence.

Spiritual wisdom is the practical application of spiritual insight. Wise believers hear the words of God and put them into practice (Matt. 7:24).

Tested faith is past experience in trusting God that leads to reliance on God's answer. Like professional athletes who practice daily to stay sharp in their sport, Christians must practice daily obeying God's Word to keep their faith sharp in daily living.

Consistent lifestyle is the result of a life lived with total allegiance to God. Spiritual maturity brings singular focus on the Lord as our source of value, inspiration, opinion, and desire. The hope and expectation is that the deacon's walk backs his talk.

New believers need to learn a different way of living. We know the simple steps that lead us into maturity as believers: a daily devotional time, a prayer and accountability partner, and a teachable spirit. Spiritual maturity defeats worldliness every time.

Key 2. Servanthood is the antidote for power struggles.

Power is the ability to act at will and to control the situation at hand. Power includes special privilege and authority. Power struggles are noticed when debate over control, authority, and privilege occur in the church. The major symptoms of power struggles are control, competition, and prestige.

Underlying the symptoms of power struggles is an unsettled acceptance of the supremacy of God over the church and the acceptance of a submissive spirit surrendered to God's leadership. The key to solving power struggles is servanthood. Servanthood is the spirit of mutual submission to one another as Christ commanded to bring glory to His name. Consider some factors present in servanthood.

Servants share; they're generous. Even an act as simple as surrendering a seat for a visitor sends a message that the members are servant-focused and not self-focused.

An elderly deacon sat on the front pew of the church during youth night; and to everyone's total surprise, he sang, clapped, and even participated in a song with hand motions. He transformed a typical youth-led service into an unforgettable night. It's not often that you see a formal Baptist deacon in a traditional church waving his hands with a worship leader wearing jeans and a T-shirt.

Several members jokingly asked him if he was changing his worship preference. "No, but tonight wasn't about me. It was about these precious students and God. So I decided that if God wants me to be an encourager this way, then bring on the bongos!"

A man of God who sets his personal preferences aside paints a picture of Christlike generosity.

Servanthood is partnership. Servants allow others to join in being part of the solution. A pastor with a servant heart encourages deacons to work with him and includes them in his leading. Deacons with servant hearts include church members in ministry. In the partnership, servants communicate respect and value for the partners they include.

Servanthood is dynamic leadership. Servants invite others to share in leadership roles. Servants do not always need to be the leader. Like a formation of geese flying south, the lead changes and they work together. All advance because all share in leading and following.

Servants enlist others to offer their thoughts and opinions. They communicate openly. They listen as well as speak. In the presence of servants, everyone feels open to sharing.

Servants trust and support one another. They enjoy community and fellowship. Servants emphasize teamwork instead of being the boss. Servants exhibit community when they adopt the attitude of "when one wins, everyone wins."

We can encourage servanthood by:
- Having a pastor and deacons who lead by example.
- Emphasizing deacon service outside of monthly meetings.
- Aiming short-term projects to meet the needs of others.
- Participating in short-term courses that enhance servanthood.

Servanthood helps solve power struggles. Rarely do you find a church on mission for God immersed in a power struggle. There's simply no time for it.

One church several years ago found itself embroiled in bitterness and contention based almost entirely on leadership issues. Men and women—lifelong members—turned monthly business meetings into opportunities to conspire, ridicule, and usurp the leaders. In one meeting a deacon and another man came so close to exchanging blows that they had to be physically restrained. The pastor and a few members prayed for God to do something—anything—to break the stronghold of rebellion and dissension. Strangely, God's answer came in the form of vandalism as a gang broke in and destroyed windows and defaced the walls of the church. God used this terrible violation. The members began to work side-by-side to restore the church facility, and in the midst of their struggle, service, and sacrifice, hearts were mended and leadership struggles began to disappear. That spirit of servanthood continued as they began to minister to the kids of their community.

Servants allow others to join in being part of the solution.

Key 3. Accountability lessens inadequate performance.
The inadequate performance of volunteers plagues many churches. Church members may promise to take an assignment never to follow through. Symptoms of inadequate performance include talk without action, unreliable service, burnout, complaints, and guilt.

Accountability lessens inadequate performance. Accountability is the awareness of being answerable to God and to His people for one's responsibility. In the parable of the talents, everyone is called into account for the stewardship of the resources entrusted to them. The seven churches of Revelation were held accountable for their response to their situations. Consider these major evidences of accountability.

Establish a customer mind-set. Leaders who are accountable ask how church members perceive the ministry and service; choices about ministry are not made according to the whim or dream of the leader. Choices are based on needs. "May I help you, please" should be the common approach in church work.

Inspect the progress of ministry teams. All ministry teams should value reporting their efforts to serve. Frequent reporting encourages everyone to work more faithfully.

Gather feedback. Congregational suggestions of needed ministries on a regular basis are essential to stay in touch with the needs of the people. Needs change, and so should the ministry offered.

Establish public goals for future work. Public goals increase efforts to achieve more for the kingdom. Annual planning based on goals mutually established by the congregation and the leaders increases cooperation and understanding as believers work toward the same destiny.

Key 4. Modeling is the solution to correcting poor examples.
Many churches have difficulty asking for improved ministry because they have never seen a better example. A new deacon fails to improve the existing deacon ministry because he imitates what he sees in the existing deacons. Sunday School teachers may be unreliable because they imitate other teachers who are poor examples. Ministry is best learned by imitation. Poor examples exist when any pattern of Christian ministry fails to reveal the standards set forth by God. Symptoms of poor examples include inconsistent lifestyles, unbiblical standards, and weak commitments.

Ministry is best learned by imitation.

Three major consequences of poor examples are that effective ministry styles are never learned, ineffective ministry is perpetuated, and improvement is difficult to comprehend. Poor examples can communicate that we can't do any better.

Modeling is the solution to poor examples. Modeling is offering a good example for others to follow. Jesus used modeling in His teaching style. Paul repeatedly referred to his own example for others to follow. Both Jesus and Paul modeled examples that have raised the bar of expectation. We need more teaching through example today. Deacons should be an example of responsible Christian lifestyles that others can imitate and thus improve in their service to God.

How can we tell if effective modeling is happening? First, we'll see leaders do what they expect from others. Our leaders will include others in their activities to teach them about the ministry. Also, being an example will be considered as important as performing a service. Deacons understand that one of their major responsibilities is to give a high standard of care for the congregation to see, to admire, and to imitate. Good models focus on living like Jesus. Consideration of the question, "What would Jesus do?" reflects the mind-set of Christians who give a model for others to respect and follow. The standard is not other deacons; it is the Lord. As a result of observing this modeling, standards are held high for the benefit of those who watch and follow.

How can we encourage modeling?

Establish written expectations of leaders in the church. Both qualifications and expectations of deacons should be approved by the church and shared each year when deacon elections are scheduled.

Publicly affirm good examples of ministry. Good ministry will inspire others to be more dedicated. Don't limit praise to deacons. Affirm everyone involved on a ministry team.

Encourage church members to work with deacons in ministry. The 20-year-old college student who works alongside two older deacons might just become a deacon in a few years. What a great opportunity for the deacons to share their passion and purpose! Good modeling helps correct poor examples.

Key 5. Emphasize multiplication to counter the lack of workers.

Many churches face critical limits on the ministry that can be performed because of too few workers. Public announcements of needs

> **Deacons should be an example of responsible Christian lifestyles that others can imitate and thus improve in their service to God.**

may yield few volunteers. Criticism about inadequate service is heard from those who do little themselves. Having too few workers frequently results in burnout, understaffed ministries, a poor response to known needs, and spectator mind-set.

Having too few workers results in significant consequences. Ministry fails to expand. So much energy is spent on maintenance of existing ministry that no new work is ever considered because the present workforce feels overworked.

Ministry teams can develop a pessimistic mind-set. A lack of enthusiasm and a spirit of complaint is a typical attitude of those who work but cannot meet all the needs. Everyone feels some frustration. Both leaders and members sense something should be done and often have negative expressions about what is done. Everyone wishes something could change, but everyone knows they can't do it with the workforce they have.

What is the solution to a lack of team members? Multiplication. Multiplication is the ability to replicate a desired lifestyle in such a way that it continues to reproduce in quality and quantity of workers. On-the-job training allowing church members to accompany deacons at work will enhance the multiplication process. Part of deacon ministry results in offering on-the-job training and encouraging others to join in ministry.

Key 6. Affirmation encourages people to continue to serve.
People do what is rewarded. Their own personal satisfaction will be reward enough for most people, but everyone likes to hear that what they do is noticed and appreciated. More affirmation of existing workers to let them know they are appreciated results in more workers and in better workers.

Activities to affirm and recognize service include an annual deacon's banquet, an annual confirmation of deacons' service, recognition of outstanding service in ministry areas—not just among deacons, a monthly celebration of ministry, and public endorsement of ministries by the pastor. Emphasis in deacons meetings needs to be both a celebration of the work performed and an encouragement to continue.

Which of these six keys does your deacon ministry team do well? _____

Which areas need improvement? _____

_____

Mobilizing for Ministry Includes All Believers

All churches need to offer ministry opportunities to all believers to live out their lives as imitations of Christ to the world. Volunteering for ministry is a personal responsibility. By encouraging each person to assume responsibility for his actions and by eliminating problems that discourage believers from service, more ministry can be accomplished.

All churches need to offer ministry opportunities to all believers to live out their lives as imitations of Christ to the world.

Team Tools

The Process for Discovering My Ministry

The following chart represent sources that can lead you to your ministry.

Spiritual gifts—gifts God gives through His Holy Spirit to empower you for service

Talents—natural abilities revealed in your physical, psychological, or emotional makeup, such as musical talent

Skills—learned ability through specialized training or education

Passion—enthusiasm God has put in your heart for a certain ministry to others

Ministries Our Church Offers

Use this form to list all ministries your church currently provides. It is more important to list all ministries than to be concerned with the appropriate category. List each ministry only once.

Intellectual Needs

Emotional Needs

Physical Needs

Spiritual Needs

Social Needs

Needs Our Church Discovered

The deacons of our church wish to identify needs in our church and community that our church can address. Listed below are types of needs that might be present. This survey will be used to continue existing ministries and to develop new ministries in the future. Please complete this survey and return it as soon as possible.

Please check all needs you feel our church should meet.

_____ Coping with stress

_____ Relationships

_____ Managing money

_____ Prayer needs

_____ Bible study skills

_____ Childcare

_____ Care for aging parents

_____ Alcohol and drug abuse

_____ Parenting problems

_____ New member orientation

_____ Divorce recovery

_____ Grief recovery

_____ Shut-in ministry

_____ Hospital ministry

_____ Reclamation of inactive members

_____ Jail ministry

_____ Marriage enrichment

_____ Public relations

_____ Crisis ministry

_____ Big brother/big sister program

_____ Disaster relief

_____ Greeters and hospitality

_____ Witnessing

_____ Other _____

_____ Other _____

_____ Other _____

Needs Our Church Identified for Attention

Use this form to compile all ministries members of the congregation indicated are current needs. List both needs that are currently being addressed as well as possible new ministry areas. It is more important to list all ministries than to be concerned with the appropriate category. List each ministry only once.

Intellectual Needs

Emotional Needs

Physical Needs

Spiritual Needs

Social Needs

Unmet Needs Our Church Identified

Use this form to compile all ministries members of the congregation indicated are current needs that are *not* currently being addressed. It is more important to list all ministries than to be concerned with the appropriate category. List each ministry only once.

Intellectual Needs

Emotional Needs

Physical Needs

Spiritual Needs

Social Needs

Need Analysis

When a ministry is proposed, it should fit the purpose and vision of the church. It should have at least two people who feel gifted and called to begin a team to meet this need. Use this form to analyze potential new ministries.

What is the need?

In what way does this potential ministry fit the purpose of the church?

In what way does this potential ministry fit the vision of the church?

Who feels led to lead this ministry?

What training, money, and other resources are needed to begin this ministry?

Spiritual Gifts Survey

Directions

This is not a test, so there are no wrong answers. The Spiritual Gifts Survey consists of 80 statements. Some items reflect concrete actions; other items are descriptive traits; and still others are statements of belief.

Select the one response you feel best characterizes yourself and place that number in the blank provided. Record your answer in the blank beside each item.

Do not spend too much time on any one item. Remember, it is not a test. Usually your immediate response is best.

Please give an answer for each item. Do not skip any items. Do not ask others how they are answering or how they think you should answer. Work at your own pace. Your response choices are:

> **5**—Highly characteristic of me/definitely true for me
> **4**—Most of the time this would describe me/be true for me
> **3**—Frequently characteristic of me/true for me–about 50 percent of the time
> **2**—Occasionally characteristic of me/true for me–about 25 percent of the time
> **1**—Not at all characteristic of me/definitely untrue for me

_____ 1. I have the ability to organize ideas, resources, time, and people effectively.
_____ 2. I am willing to study and prepare for the task of teaching.
_____ 3. I am able to relate the truths of God to specific situations.
_____ 4. I have a God-given ability to help others grow in their faith.
_____ 5. I possess a special ability to communicate the truth of salvation.
_____ 6. I have the ability to make critical decisions when necessary.
_____ 7. I am sensitive to the hurts of people.
_____ 8. I experience joy in meeting needs through sharing possessions.
_____ 9. I enjoy studying.
_____ 10. I have delivered God's message of warning and judgment.
_____ 11. I am able to sense the true motivation of persons and movements.
_____ 12. I have a special ability to trust God in difficult situations.
_____ 13. I have a strong desire to contribute to the establishment of new churches.
_____ 14. I take action to meet physical and practical needs rather than merely talking about or planning to help.
_____ 15. I enjoy entertaining guests in my home.
_____ 16. I can adapt my guidance to fit the maturity of those working with me.
_____ 17. I can delegate and assign meaningful work.
_____ 18. I have an ability and desire to teach.
_____ 19. I am usually able to analyze a situation correctly.

_____ 20. I have a natural tendency to encourage others.
_____ 21. I am willing to take the initiative in helping other Christians grow in their faith.
_____ 22. I have an acute awareness of the emotions of other people, such as loneliness, pain, fear, and anger.
_____ 23. I am a cheerful giver.
_____ 24. I spend time digging into facts.
_____ 25. I feel that I have a message from God to deliver to others.
_____ 26. I can recognize when a person is genuine/honest.
_____ 27. I am a person of vision (a clear mental portrait of a preferable future given by God). I am able to communicate vision in such a way that others commit to making the vision a reality.
_____ 28. I am willing to yield to God's will rather than question and waver.
_____ 29. I would like to be more active in getting the gospel to people in other lands.
_____ 30. It makes me happy to do things for people in need.
_____ 31. I am successful in getting a group to do its work joyfully.
_____ 32. I am able to make strangers feel at ease.
_____ 33. I have the ability to plan learning approaches.
_____ 34. I can identify those who need encouragement.
_____ 35. I have trained Christians to be more obedient disciples of Christ.
_____ 36. I am willing to do whatever it takes to see others come to Christ.
_____ 37. I am attracted to people who are hurting.
_____ 38. I am a generous giver.
_____ 39. I am able to discover new truths.
_____ 40. I have spiritual insights from Scripture concerning issues and people that compel me to speak out.
_____ 41. I can sense when a person is acting in accord with God's will.
_____ 42. I can trust in God even when things look dark.
_____ 43. I can determine where God wants a group to go and help it get there.
_____ 44. I have a strong desire to take the gospel to places where it has never been heard.
_____ 45. I enjoy reaching out to new people in my church and community.
_____ 46. I am sensitive to the needs of people.
_____ 47. I have been able to make effective and efficient plans for accomplishing the goals of a group.
_____ 48. I often am consulted when fellow Christians are struggling to make difficult decisions.
_____ 49. I think about how I can comfort and encourage others in my congregation.
_____ 50. I am able to give spiritual direction to others.

_____ 51. I am able to present the gospel to lost persons in such a way that they accept the Lord and His salvation.

_____ 52. I possess an unusual capacity to understand the feelings of those in distress.

_____ 53. I have a strong sense of stewardship based on the recognition that God owns all things.

_____ 54. I have delivered to other persons messages that have come directly from God.

_____ 55. I can sense when a person is acting under God's leadership.

_____ 56. I try to be in God's will continually and be available for His use.

_____ 57. I feel that I should take the gospel to people who have different beliefs from me.

_____ 58. I have an acute awareness of the physical needs of others.

_____ 59. I am skilled in setting forth positive and precise steps of action.

_____ 60. I like to meet visitors at church and make them feel welcome.

_____ 61. I explain Scripture in such a way that others understand it.

_____ 62. I can usually see spiritual solutions to problems.

_____ 63. I welcome opportunities to help people who need comfort, consolation, encouragement, and counseling.

_____ 64. I feel at ease in sharing Christ with nonbelievers.

_____ 65. I can influence others to perform to their highest God-given potential.

_____ 66. I recognize the signs of stress and distress in others.

_____ 67. I desire to give generously and unpretentiously to worthwhile projects and ministries.

_____ 68. I can organize facts into meaningful relationships.

_____ 69. God gives me messages to deliver to His people.

_____ 70. I am able to sense whether people are being honest when they tell of their religious experiences.

_____ 71. I enjoy presenting the gospel to persons of other cultures and backgrounds.

_____ 72. I enjoy doing little things that help people.

_____ 73. I can give a clear, uncomplicated presentation.

_____ 74. I have been able to apply biblical truth to the specific needs of my church.

_____ 75. God has used me to encourage others to live Christlike lives.

_____ 76. I have sensed the need to help other people become more effective in their ministries.

_____ 77. I like to talk about Jesus to those who do not know Him.

_____ 78. I have the ability to make strangers feel comfortable in my home.

_____ 79. I have a wide range of study resources and know how to secure information.

_____ 80. I feel assured that a situation will change for the glory of God even when the situation seem impossible.

Scoring Your Survey

Follow these directions to figure your score for each spiritual gift.

1. Place in each box your numerical response (1-5) to the item number which is indicated below the box.
2. For each gift, add the numbers in the boxes and put the total in the TOTAL box.

LEADERSHIP ___ +	___ +	___ +	___ +	___ =	___
Item 6	Item 16	Item 27	Item 43	Item 65	TOTAL
ADMINISTRATION ___ +	___ +	___ +	___ +	___ =	___
Item 1	Item 17	Item 31	Item 47	Item 59	TOTAL
TEACHING ___ +	___ +	___ +	___ +	___ =	___
Item 2	Item 18	Item 33	Item 61	Item 73	TOTAL
KNOWLEDGE ___ +	___ +	___ +	___ +	___ =	___
Item 9	Item 24	Item 39	Item 68	Item 79	TOTAL
WISDOM ___ +	___ +	___ +	___ +	___ =	___
Item 3	Item 19	Item 48	Item 62	Item 74	TOTAL
PROPHECY ___ +	___ +	___ +	___ +	___ =	___
Item 10	Item 25	Item 40	Item 54	Item 69	TOTAL
DISCERNMENT ___ +	___ +	___ +	___ +	___ =	___
Item 11	Item 26	Item 41	Item 55	Item 70	TOTAL
EXHORTATION ___ +	___ +	___ +	___ +	___ =	___
Item 20	Item 34	Item 49	Item 63	Item 75	TOTAL
SHEPHERDING ___ +	___ +	___ +	___ +	___ =	___
Item 4	Item 21	Item 35	Item 50	Item 76	TOTAL
FAITH ___ +	___ +	___ +	___ +	___ =	___
Item 12	Item 28	Item 42	Item 56	Item 80	TOTAL
EVANGELISM ___ +	___ +	___ +	___ +	___ =	___
Item 5	Item 36	Item 51	Item 64	Item 77	TOTAL
APOSTLESHIP ___ +	___ +	___ +	___ +	___ =	___
Item 13	Item 29	Item 44	Item 57	Item 71	TOTAL
SERVICE/HELPS ___ +	___ +	___ +	___ +	___ =	___
Item 14	Item 30	Item 46	Item 58	Item 72	TOTAL
MERCY ___ +	___ +	___ +	___ +	___ =	___
Item 7	Item 22	Item 37	Item 52	Item 66	TOTAL
GIVING ___ +	___ +	___ +	___ +	___ =	___
Item 8	Item 23	Item 38	Item 53	Item 67	TOTAL
HOSPITALITY ___ +	___ +	___ +	___ +	___ =	___
Item 15	Item 32	Item 45	Item 60	Item 78	TOTAL

Score

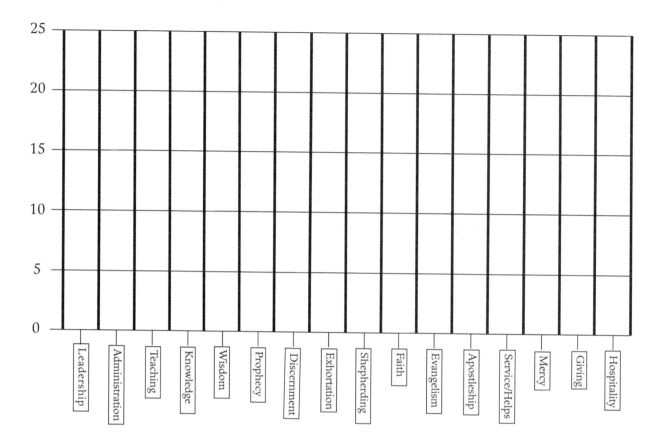

Graphing Your Profile

1. For each gift place a mark across the bar at the point that corresponds to your TOTAL for that gift.
2. For each gift shade the bar below the mark that you have drawn.
3. The resultant graph gives a picture of your gifts. Gifts for which the bars are tall are the ones in which you appear to be strongest. Gifts for which the bars are very short are the ones in which you appear not to be strong. For a definition of each gift, turn to pages 84-85.

Now that you have completed the survey, thoughtfully answer the following questions. The gifts I have begun to discover in my life are:

1. _____

2. _____

3. _____

❏ After prayer and worship, I am beginning to sense that God wants me to use my spiritual gifts to serve Christ's body by . . .

❏ I am not sure yet how God wants me to use my gifts to serve others. But I am committed to prayer and worship, seeking wisdom and opportunities to use the gifts I have received from God.

Ask God to help you know how He has gifted you for service, and how you can begin to use this gift in ministry to others.

Summary
- Spiritual gifts are God's way of empowering members of Christ's body for ministry.
- God has gifted you with a spiritual gift to empower you for ministry to others.
- The church can function according to the biblical pattern revealed in the Antioch church (Acts 13:1-3) by: (1) observing and recognizing the spiritual giftedness of its members; (2) hearing God's call to set members aside for service; (3) setting members aside for their place of service and empowering them to perform that ministry.
- God gifted you for His glory, not your gain.

Definitions/Explanations of Spiritual Gifts

A spiritual gift is an expression of the Holy Spirit in the life of believers which empowers them to serve the body of Christ, the church.

Write your own definition of "spiritual gift" in the margin.

Romans 12:6-8; 1 Corinthians 12:8-10,28-30; Ephesians 4:11; and 1 Peter 4:9-11 contain representative lists of gifts and roles God has given to the church. A definition of these gifts follows.

Leadership—Leadership aids the body by leading and directing members to accomplish the goals and purposes of the church. Leadership motivates people to work together in unity toward common goals (Rom. 12:8).

Administration—Persons with the gift of administration lead the body by steering others to remain on task. Administration enables the body to organize according to God-given purposes and long-term goals (1 Cor. 12:28).

Teaching—Teaching is instructing members in the truths and doctrines of God's Word for the purposes of building up, unifying, and maturing the body (1 Cor. 12:28; Rom. 12:7; Eph. 4:11).

Knowledge—The gift of knowledge manifests itself in teaching and training in discipleship. It is the God-given ability to learn, know, and explain the precious truths of God's Word. A word of knowledge is a Spirit-revealed truth (1 Cor. 12:28).

Wisdom—Wisdom is the gift that discerns the work of the Holy Spirit in the body and applies His teachings and actions to the needs of the body (1 Cor. 12:28).

Prophecy—The gift of prophecy is proclaiming the Word of God boldly. This builds up the body and leads to conviction of sin. Prophecy manifests itself in preaching and teaching (1 Cor. 12:10; Rom. 12:6).

Discernment—Discernment aids the body by recognizing the true intentions of those within or related to the body. Discernment tests the message and actions of others for the protection and well-being of the body (1 Cor. 12:10).

Exhortation—Possessors of this gift encourage members to be involved in and enthusiastic about the work of the Lord. Members with this gift are good counselors and motivate others to service. Exhortation exhibits itself in preaching, teaching, and ministry (Rom. 12:8).

Shepherding—The gift of shepherding is manifested in persons who look out for the spiritual welfare of others. Although pastors, like shepherds, do care for members of the church, this gift is not limited to a pastor or staff member (Eph. 4:11).

Faith—Faith trusts God to work beyond the human capabilities of the people.

Believers with this gift encourage others to trust in God in the face of apparently insurmountable odds (1 Cor. 12:9).

Evangelism—God gifts his church with evangelists to lead others to Christ effectively and enthusiastically. This gift builds up the body by adding new members to its fellowship (Eph. 4:11).

Apostleship—The church sends apostles from the body to plant churches or be missionaries. Apostles motivate the body to look beyond its walls in order to carry out the Great Commission (1 Cor. 12:28; Eph. 4:11).

Service/Helps—Those with the gift of service/helps recognize practical needs in the body and joyfully give assistance to meeting those needs. Christians with this gift do not mind working behind the scenes (1 Cor. 12:28; Rom. 12:7).

Mercy—Cheerful acts of compassion characterize those with the gift of mercy. Persons with this gift aid the body by empathizing with hurting members. They keep the body healthy and unified by keeping others aware of the needs within the church (Rom. 12:8).

Giving—Members with the gift of giving give freely and joyfully to the work and mission of the body. Cheerfulness and liberality are characteristics of individuals with this gift (Rom. 12:8).

Hospitality—Those with this gift have the ability to make visitors, guests, and strangers feel at ease. They often use their home to entertain guests. Persons with this gift integrate new members into the body (1 Pet. 4:9).

God has gifted you with an expression of His Holy Spirit to support His vision and mission of the church. It is a worldwide vision to reach all people with the gospel of Christ. As a servant leader, God desires that you know how He has gifted you. This will lead you to where He would have you serve as part of His vision and mission for the church.

Summary
- Servant leaders continue to learn how God has gifted them for service.
- To receive God's grace for salvation is to receive God's gift for service in Christ's body.
- The church is a living body, unified in purpose while diverse in its parts.
- Every member belongs to the body.
- Spiritual gifts are for the common good of God's vision and mission for the church.
- A spiritual gift is an expression of the Holy Spirit which empowers each member for service. God desires that you know how He has gifted you.

Questions and Answers About Deacon Ministry Teams

Following are some questions and answers that might help you in developing deacon ministry teams based on spiritual gifts.

Why are deacons considering the deacon ministry teams over other styles of deacon ministry currently being performed in churches?
Deacons are considering developing deacon ministry teams because they provide a way for deacons to serve, to use their gifts in ministry. Many churches are turning to a team approach that focuses on ministry rather than control. Deacon ministry teams allow for a diversification of roles and ministries. This approach to ministry also provides an avenue for church members to assist in specific ministries.

How are deacons assigned to/selected for a specific ministry?
A combination of a deacon's spiritual gifts and the deacon's personal preference for specific ministries should be the basis for selection. Each deacon should be able to volunteer for a ministry that feels like a calling from God or a passion in his life. When in doubt about the assignment of a deacon, the deacon himself should make the call. He is the only one who knows what God is calling him to do.

How long are ministry assignments for each deacon?
Ministry assignments last for one year or as long as the need exists. If a need is satisfied before the year is complete, the deacon will be encouraged to make another selection and move to another ministry team.

Why is it considered better for a deacon to volunteer for a ministry than to be appointed?
No one knows the passion or calling of a person better than the person himself. The deacon ministry leadership team (deacon leaders or officers) may make many wise decisions, but no assignment process will satisfy every deacon unless each can participate in

the process of ministry assignments. A deacon who volunteers for a ministry team will have a greater ownership.

How many deacons are needed in a church to perform this type of deacon ministry?

Each church should continue with the same criteria it has been using to determine the number of deacons needed. The number of deacons is not as important as that all are called to minister. When church members serve with the deacons in the various functions, more ministry can be accomplished.

How many deacons are needed for each ministry to be covered?

At least two people should be assigned to any ministry attempted. Some ministries in the church will be led by deacons. Other ministries may have teams comprised of Sunday School classes, women's groups, mission groups, or others. On a deacon ministry team, at least one member should be a deacon so the ministry can be accountable to the deacons. The deacon may or may not be the team leader.

There are two reasons to recommend at least two people per ministry. First, two people prevent one person being overwhelmed by the need. Second, two people call for accountability from each other. Two or more people can support and encourage one another. As many believers as desire to serve in an area may be allowed on the same team.

Is deacon rotation in this system of ministry?

The current policy of deacon rotation in a church can continue. If no rotation of deacons is functioning, a rotation of the team leaders in ministry should occur.

If deacons consider developing deacon ministry teams, how many ministries should be attempted in the beginning?

No set number of ministries is suggested. Each situation will be different. Enough options should be offered so that each deacon may find an area of ministry that allows him to use his gifts. The number of options should be small enough to ensure coordination and implementation.

Once the needs surveys are complete, deacons can begin to determine how many ministries to begin. Some ministries will require more time and effort than others. Consider the demands of each ministry when determining how many to begin. It is far better to begin a few ministries and do those well. Other ministries can be developed in the future. Build on your successes.

If our deacons cannot perform every ministry needed, how do we set priorities?
Priorities may be set by two criteria. The most important factor may be the critical needs in the fellowship. Listen to what the members are saying about needed ministries. The second factor may be the passion or calling of the deacons. God calls persons into service because He knows that their unique contribution will be needed. Many ministries of the church will continue and be started without deacons. When deacons see needs they do not have men or other resources to address, they should turn the need over to the congregation to lead and staff.

May an inactive deacon continue to serve in a ministry responsibility?
An inactive deacon is encouraged to continue to serve in any ministry he feels called to do.

May a deacon serve in more than one specific ministry area?
Deacons may serve in more than one area. Care should be taken to protect deacons from exhaustion by having too many functions at once.

How and when should deacon ministry team leaders be selected?
Team leaders should be selected according to the normal procedure of the church in electing deacon ministry team leaders. The process is the same as your church has previously used.

How and when are team leaders selected?
Ministry team leaders are selected by the team itself when enough people are gathered to form a team to meet a ministry need. People who have gifts of administration or leadership may be enlisted to serve as team leader.

How are job descriptions, policies, and procedures for specific ministries approved?
Job descriptions are created from the team responsible for that particular ministry. Policies and procedures can originate from the deacon ministry team, team leaders, or the ministry teams. The entire deacon ministry team may choose to review and approve all job descriptions, policies and procedures for accountability purposes. The reason for this accountability is to reduce conflicts between teams and to ensure that every deacon is aware of the entire deacon ministry.

What is the role of the pastor in relation to deacons in deacon team ministry?
The pastor is considered part of the team attempting to meet the needs of the church members. He should be considered the shepherd and leader of pastoral ministries. In

keeping with Ephesians 4:11-13, the pastor should be perceived as the equipper of the deacons and the church for the work of ministry. As deacons identify the ministries they wish to perform, the pastor should help them find appropriate training and literature that will adequately prepare the teams for ministry. The pastor can provide on-the-job training by including a deacon with him on many pastoral duties. This is a wonderful way to equip deacons to be partners in pastoral ministry.

What is the relationship of church members to deacons in the deacon team ministry?

Church members are encouraged to serve alongside deacons, helping to perform the ministry. Members should be encouraged to volunteer for ministries that are consistent with their spiritual gifts and interests. Ministering to the needs of the church should be perceived as a churchwide responsibility.

How should deacons in deacon team ministry relate to ongoing ministries and other teams of the church?

The team ministry of deacons should have the purpose of filling the gaps in ministry. If another group is currently fulfilling a need, deacons should not compete. A focus of the most efficient way to meet needs should guide all decisions regarding new ministry.

When should the spiritual gifts inventory be administered?

Administer the inventory before or during orientation prior to the first deacons meeting of the new year. This option would allow all dimensions of orientation to be handled at one time.

How often should deacons take the spiritual gifts inventory?

Deacons should be encouraged to take the inventory each time they are reactivated as deacons. Some deacons might even wish to take the inventory each year.

Why should a deacon take the inventory more than once?

Taking the inventory more than once offers a chance for a deacon to gain additional understanding about his calling. It may be true that gifts do not change. However, our understanding of our gifts might change with experience and spiritual maturity. A deacon should take the inventory every time he is reactivated as a deacon.

How is training accomplished for so many varied tasks?

Training opportunities will be offered at various times and places according to the needs and schedules of the deacons of each ministry team. Because training is offered for each ministry team with only a few deacons involved, fewer conflicts of schedules will occur. Additionally, more focused training on particular needs can be prepared when training is focused on one task at a time. Training can be accomplished by outside leaders, other professionals, pastor, staff ministers, other deacons, or through individual or group study. If each ministry team keeps notes from training opportunities, this information can be passed to future teams. Each team can develop a training manual for a particular ministry team.

Deacon Ministry Team Retreat/Training Event

The following is a flexible plan for a retreat or a series of meetings to help your deacon ministry team unleash the power of ministry teams. Although a retreat is preferable, the content can be covered in a number of formats such as a weekly training session or making sessions part of regular deacon ministry team meetings.

Keep in mind that this retreat plan should be used as a reinforcement and application of the principles found within the book. You will not be able to cover all of the content in *Unleashing the Power of Deacon-led Ministry Teams*. Encourage deacons to make this resource an ongoing tool as they seek to minister, lead, model, and inspire.

Plan to purchase a book for each deacon before the retreat. Urge the deacons to read the book before the retreat or to read each chapter in advance of the study if it is conducted in individual sessions.

Note to leader: Read through the book and study thoroughly this teaching plan. You'll discover that there will be items to gather for each session. Pray that God will use you to facilitate discussion and motivate deacons to capture the vision of ministry teams.

If you choose to conduct sessions in a retreat setting, you may want to lead deacons to gather information from the congregation about perceived needs in advance of the scheduled retreat.

Session 1

1. Begin this first session by asking each deacon to share the name of a person who inspired him to become a deacon. Then pray a prayer of thanksgiving for mentors and heroes among us and in heaven.
2. Discuss the section "Organized to Serve" (beginning on page 11).
3. State: Almost every church has some characteristics of both of these types of church models.
4. Ask the deacons to brainstorm where their church and the deacons fit best when thinking of these two models. Use the discussion questions on page 16 to guide the discussion. Keep the discussion informal, nonthreatening and honest.
5. Invite a volunteer to read Acts 6:1-4.

6. Summarize the author's teaching found on pages 19-21. Spend a maximum of eight minutes on this teaching. Move quickly to a time of discussion.
7. Ask the deacons to write down and then discuss the question: In your life as a believer, whom do you serve?
8. Conclude this discussion by displaying a rope made of many strands.
9. Read the passage on page 26-27 from Ecclesiastes 4. Ask the deacons to spend a few moments in prayer that God will bind them and their church like the strands of the rope.

Session 2

1. Introduce this session by stating that as a team of servants the deacon ministry team will now turn a corner in this study and evaluate where they believe the church is in terms of needs and ministries and and where they are as a deacon ministry team in terms of discerning needs and providing ministries to meet those needs.
2. Ask deacons to turn to page 73. If possible, divide into small groups to work together to complete this inventory. You may want to ask groups to move to separate rooms for their discussions. Allow enough time for the teams to complete this process. As a leader check in with each group to keep them focused on the task and to check their progress.
3. Call the small groups back into the general session area and ask each team to report. Assign a deacon to record information as it is given by writing on large sheets of paper attached to the walls. Each sheet should have one of the needs categories printed on it: emotional, intellectual, physical, spiritual, social. Receive input one sheet at a time and allow a different group an opportunity to be first in order to balance the input.
4. After this process work through the "Needs Our Church Discovered" form on page 74.

Session 3

1. Ask a deacon to pray, thanking God for the uniqueness of each person on the deacon ministry team of your church. If possible recruit this person ahead of time.
2. Begin this session by showing a video clip of a championship game such as the Super Bowl or an NCAA Championship. (You can find highlight archives of these games in almost every video rental store in the sports and special events section.) Allow your deacons to relive and enjoy this experience. Limit the video to no more than 10 minutes.

3. Ask the deacons: "What memorable sporting event comes to mind when you think about a team that excelled in camaraderie and teamwork?"

4. Leader: Share a personal story about a time when you saw teamwork happen in your church.

5. Ask someone to read Romans 12:1-8.

6. Ask: How do you see this concept within our church?

7. In 12 minutes give a brief overview of what spiritual gifts are. Use chapter 5 and the information about different gifts found in the Team Tools on pages 84-85. Other excellent resources to contribute to this discussion include C. Gene Wilkes, *Jesus on Leadership* (LifeWay Press, ISBN 0-7673-9855-6) and David Francis, *Spiritual Gifts: A Practical Guide to How God Works Through You* (LifeWay Press, ISBN 0-6330-9936-8).

8. After briefly explaining and identifying the variety of gifts and ways they might be used on ministry teams, ask the deacons to complete the survey found on pages 78-82. Use the directions at the front of the test to explain the purpose of the survey and the manner in which this inventory should be conducted.

9. Allow the deacons as much time as needed to complete the gifts inventory. (If you are not doing this in a retreat session, you may ask deacons to do the inventory at home between sessions.)

10. After the survey is completed, use sheets of construction paper and list the names and primary gifts (top 3) of each deacon, one sheet per deacon. Print the results large enough that they a readable to the entire group. As the deacons share their results allow others to respond and affirm the deacons gifts.

11. Ask: How have you already seen God use these spiritual gifts in the ministries of the people in this room?

Session 4

1. Begin this final session by showing a video of your town. This can easily be done ahead of time with a video camera. Show different parts of the neighborhoods, especially those surrounding your church. Video the bars, the schools, the softball fields, the nursing homes, the apartments. In other words, show both the good and the bad aspects about your town. This video should only last approximately three minutes.

2. After viewing the video ask: Considering everything that we have experienced through this book and this retreat, what were you thinking as you saw these familiar images?

3. Give the deacons time to respond. Guide them in their conversation to think of the opportunities that are all around them.

4. Purchase or create a large map of your town. Invite the deacons to take a sticker or

pin and mark where they live. Share with the deacons the following concept: God has placed us strategically all over this area to do His work.

5. Ask: How could God use you in your work, church, and leisure?

6. Ask three or four deacons to read aloud John 15.

7. Ask: What fruit do you think God will allow our church to bear. Urge deacons to be concrete without using vague, churchy words.

8. Record all of these thoughts on a large sheet of paper. Take time after a few thoughts are recorded to pray about the suggestions offered in this ideation session. Tell the deacons that this is not an exercise of appraising each thought or idea.

9. Briefly overview the six keys to developing a ministering church. Ask the deacons questions during this overview to access the church's progress in relation to the six keys mentioned (see pages 64-71).

10. Close this session by asking deacons to divide into two or three groups to pray for their community and the process of developing ministry teams in the days ahead.

Retreat Tips: Invite a guest to present a short devotional or testimony during the prayer breakfast. Spend the prayer time during the breakfast praying for personal needs of each deacon's family.

Recreation: This might be anything from horseshoes to table games or a wilderness hike. Do this activity together. Sometimes these moments of play do just as much for the chemistry of your deacon ministry team as the sessions themselves.

Retreat Schedule

Friday Night

5:30 p.m.	Dinner
6:30 p.m.	Session 1
7:30 p.m.	Break
7:45 p.m.	Session 2
9:00 p.m.	Dismiss

Saturday

7:30 a.m.	Prayer Breakfast
9:00 a.m.	Session 3
9:15 a.m.	Break
10:30 a.m.	Session 3 (continued)
11:30 a.m.	Lunch
12:30 p.m.	A Recreation Break
2:30 p.m.	Session 4
4:00 p.m.	Adjourn

CHRISTIAN GROWTH STUDY PLAN

In the **Christian Growth Study Plan (formerly Church Study Course),** this book *Unleashing the Power of Deacon-Led Ministry Teams* is a resource for course credit in the subject area Ministry of the Christian Growth category of plans. To receive credit, read the book, complete the learning activities, show your work to your pastor, a staff member or church leader, then complete the following information. This page may be duplicated. Send the completed page to:

Christian Growth Study Plan
• One LifeWay Plaza • Nashville, TN 37234-0117
• FAX: 615.251.5067 • Email: cgspnet@lifeway.com
For information about the Christian Growth Study Plan, refer to the Christian Growth Study Plan Catalog. It is located online at *www.lifeway.com/cgsp*. If you do not have access to the Internet, contact the Christian Growth Study Plan office (1.800.968.5519) for the specific plan you need for your ministry.

UNLEASHING THE POWER OF DEACON-LED MINISTRY TEAMS
COURSE NUMBER: LS-0529

PARTICIPANT INFORMATION

Social Security Number (USA ONLY-optional)	Personal CGSP Number*	Date of Birth (MONTH, DAY, YEAR)

Name (First, Middle, Last)

Home Phone

Address (Street, Route, or P.O. Box) | City, State, or Province | Zip/Postal Code

Please check appropriate box: ❑ Resource purchased by self ❑ Resource purchased by church ❑ Other

CHURCH INFORMATION

Church Name

Address (Street, Route, or P.O. Box) | City, State, or Province | Zip/Postal Code

CHANGE REQUEST ONLY

☐ Former Name

☐ Former Address | City, State, or Province | Zip/Postal Code

☐ Former Church | City, State, or Province | Zip/Postal Code

Signature of Pastor, Conference Leader, or Other Church Leader | Date

*New participants are requested but not required to give SS# and date of birth. Existing participants, please give CGSP# when using SS# for the first time. Thereafter, only one ID# is required. **Mail to:** Christian Growth Study Plan, One LifeWay Plaza, Nashville, TN 37234-0117. Fax: (615)251-5067.

Rev. 3-03